Idle Weeds

THE LIFE OF A SANDSTONE RIDGE

David Rains Wallace

Illustrations by Jennifer Dewey

A YOLLA BOLLY PRESS BOOK, PUBLISHED BY

Sierra Club Books   San Francisco

Printed in the United States of America.

Idle Weeds was developed and prepared for publication at
The Yolla Bolly Press, Covelo, California, under the supervision of
James and Carolyn Robertson during the fall and winter of 1979-80.
Production staff: Diana Fairbanks, Barbara Speegle, Dan Hibshman,
Joyca Cunnan, and Jim Bequette.

The Sierra Club, founded in 1892 by John Muir, has devoted itself
to the study and protection of the earth's scenic and ecological resources—
mountains, wetlands, woodlands, wild shores and rivers, deserts and plains.
Its publications are part of the nonprofit effort the club carries on as a
public trust. There are more than 50 chapters coast to coast,
in Canada, Hawaii, and Alaska. For information about how you may
participate in the club's programs to enjoy and preserve wilderness
and the quality of life, please address inquiries to: Sierra Club,
530 Bush Street, San Francisco, California 94108.

First edition

Library of Congress Cataloging in Publication Data

Wallace, David Rains, 1945-
Idle weeds.
Bibliography: p. 170
Includes index.
1. Urban ecology—Ohio. 2. Natural history—Ohio.
I. Sierra Club. II. Title.
QH105.03W34   500.9'173'3   79-21447
ISBN 0-87156-271-5

To Betsy, who was there

ACKNOWLEDGMENTS

This book would not have come about without generous assistance. Edward F. Hutchins, James Stahl, and Chris Toops shared their considerable knowledge of Ohio natural history with me, as did Ruth Melvin and her late husband Jack Melvin. Paul B. Sears and E. E. Good reviewed the manuscript and made many useful suggestions and corrections. Jim and Carolyn Robertson, Dan Hibshman, and Jon Beckmann helped tighten up some slack places in the manuscript. I take full responsibility for whatever flaws remain.

There are many Blackhand sandstone ridges along the western escarpment of the Appalachian Plateau, and this book is not a literal portrait of any particular one. It is a composite of several places I have known, held together with some degree of poetic license.

CONTENTS

PAST TIME, page 1

PRESENT TIME: A YEAR ON THE RIDGE, page 13
Snow Cover, 14
Ground Thaw, 29
Woodland Flowers, 42
Bird Songs, 60
Scrubland Flowers, 74
Wetland Flowers, 91
Insect Songs, 107
Leaf Color, 130
Hard Frost, 148

FUTURE TIME, page 163

BIBLIOGRAPHY, page 170

GLOSSARY OF PLANTS AND ANIMALS, page 173

Past Time

*The ploughed field . . . was well tilled, and nowhere was there
a blade of grass or any kind of plant to be seen, it was all
black. "Ah, what a destructive creature is man. . . . How many
different plant lives he destroys to support his own existence!"
thought I, involuntarily looking around for some living thing
in this lifeless black field. In front of me to the right of the road
I saw some kind of little clump, and drawing near I found
it was the same kind of thistle as that which I had vainly plucked
and thrown away. This "Tartar" plant had three branches.
One was broken and stuck out like the stump of a mutilated arm.
Each of the other two bore a flower, once red but now
blackened. One stalk was broken, and half of it hung down
with a soiled flower at its tip. The other, though also soiled with
black mud, still stood erect. Evidently, a cartwheel had passed
over the plant but it had risen again. . . .*

*"What vitality!" I thought. "Man has conquered everything and
destroyed millions of plants, yet this one won't submit."*

Leo Tolstoy
Hadji Murad

C HESTNUT Ridge is a place that doesn't fit easily into human plans and categories. It is a narrow outcropping of resistant sandstone, nothing unusual, but it exists on the borders of things and thus has a quality of uncertainty. It is what economists and planners call "marginal land."

The ridge is located between two very different regions of the United States and has aspects of both. Looking east from the cornfields of the central lowland, it is a line of trees slightly higher than the other woodlots; but looking west from the forested hills of the Appalachian Plateau, it is just another forested hill. It is not quite part of the Appalachian world of steep ridges and impoverished hollows, but neither is it part of the rich, level Midwest. The ridge has seen both Appalachian poverty and Midwestern affluence, and its second-growth woods include both the black and scarlet oaks of the acid hill soils and the hackberries and beeches of the limestone-based lowland soils.

Even its name is ambiguous. The American chestnut no longer grows there, having succumbed to blight in the 1930s. Endemic to Appalachia, the chestnut set the ridge somewhat apart from the lowland, whose farmers and townspeople couldn't get the sweet nuts on their own fertile lands and so had to buy them from the hill folk. But the last chestnut stump on the ridge stopped sprouting in the 1960s, and that distinction is gone.

The borderline quality of Chestnut Ridge runs deeper than geography, vegetation, and soils. Its geology and history have also been linked to borders and the uncertainties borders imply. It seems straightforward enough to pick up a piece of Blackhand sandstone, to feel its coarseness and see the orange iron oxide that cements the sand grains. A lump of sedimentary rock might seem the essence of dull certainty—mere matter clamped in the ground for inconsequential ages—but the existence of rock strata is problematic and venturesome, to say the least. Continents parade across oceans, seas roll over continents—today's sea may be tomorrow's mountaintop.

Geologists believe that Blackhand sandstone originated at the seaward border of a river delta about 330 million years ago during the Mississippian Period, when an inland sea covered the North American heartland. The river that formed the delta had its headwaters in mountains that caught large amounts of rain, resulting in frequent floods. These floods may have created Blackhand sandstone. The river usually deposited its coarse sands as it entered the lowlands; but when in flood, it washed them to the delta border, where denser salt water forced the floodwater upward. Abruptly slowed, the floods dropped the sand in deposits that eventually reached a depth of five hundred feet.

The ancient delta must have been an impressively lonely place: no sea birds called over it, no reeds or rushes waved in its winds. Not even crabs had evolved to scuttle over its sands, although there were probably trilobites and macabre-looking amphibians with saw teeth and humped backs. But Blackhand sandstone tells us very little about the delta's early denizens because virtually no fossils are preserved in it. The borderland of fresh and salt water was a difficult environment for many creatures, and the coarse sand was not favorable for fossil making. Agitated by tides and river, it ground away soft shells and bones sandpaper fashion instead of providing a bed of soft ooze as do limestone and shale sediments.

The absence of fossils also makes it hard to know how long the sands were deposited, since it is impossible to see any evolution of organisms from the bottom of this stratum to its top. The sand deposition probably stopped when the river abandoned its

3

delta, too much sediment having accumulated to allow free flow. Since floods no longer brought coarse sand, the deposits that would become Blackhand sandstone gradually disappeared under layers of mud and fine sand deposited by seashore currents. This overburden compressed the sand grains, and water full of iron oxide from organic mud residues cemented them.

The next 300 million years seem to have been sedate ones for Blackhand sandstone. It was not folded or thrust up because it lay outside the tectonic zones where the wandering of continents distorts the earth's crust. Instead it was gradually uplifted along with the rest of eastern North America, and the inland seas that had covered it retreated more or less permanently. This had the effect of not burying the Blackhand sandstone too deeply for later human acquaintance: sedimentation stops where there is no water to deposit sediment, so sedimentary rock more or less stopped being formed over Blackhand sandstone. It was covered only by a few thousand feet of late Mississippian and Pennsylvanian strata, not enough to bury it forever.

The overlying deposits—it is assumed—eroded away during the ensuing 300 million years, thus exposing the north-south tongue of sandstone called Chestnut Ridge. There is no absolute way of proving this, simply because the overlying deposits no longer exist. The assumption is based on the existence of similar deposits over Blackhand sandstone farther east. But uncertainty remains. We feel that we know the Chestnut Ridge bedrock because we can see and touch it, but because we can see it, because the rock that once covered it is gone, there is no way of knowing for certain what happened after its formation. The apparent firmness of bedrock dissolves in the vertigo of 300 million vanished years.

We can't even be sure how long Chestnut Ridge has existed because we don't know when the overlying rock eroded away. Eroded rock leaves less evidence of its earthly passage than the most ephemeral of living things; life forms may become fossils, but eroded rocks just become other rocks. Geologists might be able to identify and date bits of the shaly Logan sandstone that presumably covered Chestnut Ridge, but they would have to cover some ground to do so. Sediments holding such bits could lie anywhere from Ohio to the Mississippi delta.

The first geological certainty to touch Chestnut Ridge after the formation of its bedrock is awesome. Among the mossy chunks of sandstone on the slopes of the ridge are pieces of pinkish granite so hard that they are usually free of moss. These rocks often have a pinstripe pattern of scratches on their flat surfaces. Other pieces of granite, equally hard, made the scratches as the Wisconsin Glacier dragged these igneous rocks southward from their origins in central Canada. Geologists believe the continental ice sheet covered the area for perhaps a hundred thousand years and retreated only fifteen thousand years ago.

Chestnut Ridge must have existed when the Wisconsin Glacier covered Ohio, because it was clearly an obstacle to the advancing ice. A heap of glacial drift—soil, pebbles, and rocks carved by the glacier—is piled against the ridge's west slope, an indication that the glacier's front paused there for some time. The drift was deposited against the ridge as silt is deposited upstream of a dam. The east slope lacks this heap of glacial drift and thus is much steeper than the west. Eventually the ice did spill over the ridge, but it must have been slowed and thinned. The glacier did not extend more than a few dozen miles southeast of the ridge.

After seeing the deep glacial gorges of western mountains, one might wonder why the Wisconsin glaciation didn't simply shave Chestnut Ridge down to valley level and clank away south carrying it in pieces. The continental ice sheet lacked the force that gravity gives to mountain glaciers, and it was lighter and shallower around its borders than in its interior. So Chestnut Ridge was only banked and glazed with drift, not leveled or buried. Typically, it came to have features of both glaciated and unglaciated landscapes. Oak and chestnut grew best on the steep, acid east slope, while beech and maple thrived where glacial drift buried the sandstone.

The glaciers seem catastrophic to us, but they were not really different in kind from the forces that formed Blackhand sandstone and carved Chestnut Ridge from it. The flow of ice crystals is merely a variation of the flow of floodwaters or raindrops. A more catastrophic event struck the ridge after the ice sheet had retreated; in fact, the glacier helped bring about the event by leaving behind its fertile till plain to the west. The rich, calcareous soil and abundant groundwater of the lowland fostered civilization, a geological force that would carve away more of Chestnut Ridge in a hundred years than rain and ice had removed in thousands.

The first sign of human activity on Chestnut Ridge dates from perhaps two thousand years ago and consists of a few low, earthen mounds, which an Amerindian people called the Woodland Culture may have built. This people lived in bark houses, grew vegetables, and built mounds in many parts of the Midwest and Appalachia, usually over graves and presumably for religious reasons. The Chestnut Ridge mounds haven't been excavated by archeologists, though, so the reason for their existence is uncertain. A trench dug into one mound by an amateur yielded only Blackhand sandstone. The mound might have been made by a farmer clearing stones from a cornfield for all anyone knows.

Whatever their origin, the mounds are largely undistinguishable from the rest of the ridge except for one particular: perhaps because their soil is deeper, they grow more wildflowers than other ground. In early spring the trenched mound is covered with white bloodroot and spring beauty blossoms, while in late August another mound supports a patch of Jerusalem artichoke, a tall sunflower. Jerusalem artichoke was probably a food plant of the Woodland Indians. The flower-covered mounds are like memorials to that vanished people, who seem to have treated the ridge rather gently. They got their living in the rich valleys and had no need to tear up the hills for timber, minerals, or farmland. A virgin forest probably covered the ridge until white settlement in the early nineteenth century.

The nature of that virgin forest is uncertain as well. It has long since disappeared into the buildings and fireplaces of the countryside. Two huge beeches on the south slope may have been part of the original forest. Beeches are usually the oldest trees in farm woods because they make inferior timber and provide shade and beechnuts for livestock. A chestnut stump almost four feet across on the east slope may have produced nuts that fed passenger pigeons in its day, although it is too rotten to read its age from growth rings. The stump is surrounded by three smaller chestnut stumps, sprouts that grew from the parent stump after it was cut and were themselves cut when they reached maturity. None of the other ridge trees are much more than a hundred years old. The removal of the virgin forest was particularly complete on the gentle, fertile west slope, which was converted to orchards, pastures, and fields.

The steeper south, east, and north slopes would probably have been deforested as completely as the west if the Blackhand sandstone had not attracted the builders of a nearby canal around 1835. Canals were the freeways of the period, and there was a rush to build them. Roads were pushed up the ridge slopes, and soil was torn off and flung downhill in great heaps that remain, tree covered, to this day. Hundreds of massive blocks were hewn from the sandstone, carted into the valley, and built into canal locks by Irish laborers who are said to have died like flies from typhoid in the process. Fifteen years later the railroads came, and the canals were abandoned. The quarries were useless for farming and were allowed to revert to second-growth forest.

There is almost no sign of the canal in the valley today, but the Blackhand locks, although they now stand among pawpaw trees in a floodplain woodland quite apart from human activity, are as firm as the day they were built. A large sycamore has grown between two blocks, and its white roots erupting from the worked stone recall the Mayan cities of the Peten. On Chestnut Ridge big sycamores, black cherries, sugar maples, and beeches grow even in the deepest quarry pit, where a cliff about thirty feet high keeps out sunlight for all but a few hours of the day. Because of the trees, the casual observer is unaware that the cliffs are man-made. The only discernible mark of civilization on them is some names carved in 1870.

Quarrying seems to have been the only industrial influence on the ridge. Afterwards, the agricultural deterioration that afflicted most of the Appalachian plateau ran its course. Exposed by plowing and grazing, the thin, nutrient-poor ridge soils crept quietly downhill or hurried away into gullies. In the second half of the nineteenth century when lowland farmers were building barns and houses, people on the ridges were still living in log cabins chinked with plaster. A 1907 geological survey map shows a dwelling on Chestnut Ridge that could be reached only

7

by a foot path. No trace of this cabin remains today, but pieces of split-rail fence on the south slope may have been contemporaneous.

The cabin dwellers probably drifted away to lowland cities, leaving the ridge to more prosperous landowners. In 1918 a man returned from army service in the Pacific, bought a chunk of the ridge, and planted apple orchards. Various other land improvement projects marked the first half of the twentieth century. Owners planted pines, black locusts, and tulip trees on gullied slopes, plowed steep fields to contour, fenced or hedged their pastures, and dug fish ponds. People built pleasant houses on a gravel township road along the west slope.

But this improved rural world also deteriorated after 1950, not from poverty but from affluence. Children who had grown up in the pleasant houses found interests elsewhere, and land speculators from the exploding city on the western horizon began eyeing the ridge. The man who had planted the apple orchards now drenched them in lead arsenate, DDT, and parathion in an attempt to compete in an increasingly fastidious and mechanized market. Dumps of plastic throwaway containers appeared in the carefully fenced fields and pastures, now abandoned and growing into thickets of elm and ash. Chestnut Ridge became a weekend resort: townspeople bought parcels and put trailers or cabins on them.

When the old apple farmer died, a developer bought his land and began selling subdivided lots, which he advertised as "a delightful, unspoiled sylvan setting for quality homes." He proposed to build the homes, too, and had begun digging foundations when the regional park agency bought him out. The agency had acquired land from sympathetic owners at the south end of the ridge and was gingerly buying its way north. By 1970 it controlled the ridge.

The developers turned their attention elsewhere, and the park agency quietly removed the weekend cabins and trailers and discouraged some off-road motorcyclists who had begun tearing up the ridgetop. It leased the small area of nonabandoned pasture and meadow to a local cattle raiser, and the township road remained a favorite haunt of beer drinkers, backseat lovers, marijuana smokers, trash dumpers, and mushroom pickers. Except for these visitors, the ridge was left undisturbed until the typically underfunded park agency could raise sufficient money to install paved roads, playgrounds, picnic areas, a nature center, a sledding hill, a boating lake, and whatever other facilities were required to justify leaving it in a natural state.

For a little while, then, Chestnut Ridge could be simply itself, a miniscule part of the biosphere without much pretense to economic, scientific, or recreational value. Of course, it made no difference to the ridge whether civilization used it as a park or a housing development for one or two ticks of its geological clock's secondhand. But this benign neglect offered an opportunity to observe the ridge as one might watch a wild animal that had been kept captive, then allowed to run loose again. One could watch as the movements became feral and the eyes were rekindled with some of the old light of independence.

The nature of the beast is not an altogether ingratiating one. The ridge is somewhat the worse for wear and presents itself accordingly. If it could be compared to any single animal species, it would have to be to the one that has dug itself in and hung on the hardest there—the groundhog.

Events at a house on the ridge illustrate the tenacity of the groundhog. An individual groundhog dug a den beside the concrete foundation—an unsightly addition, which the occupants decided to remove. They live-trapped the groundhog, exiled it to the next county, and filled in the burrow, but in some mysterious way the site had become prime groundhog real estate. Another groundhog promptly redug the burrow, was trapped in its turn, and then replaced by yet another groundhog.

The house began to attract an inexhaustible supply of groundhogs. When its occupants started gassing them in the burrow, the next groundhog would simply fling the decayed carcass of its predecessor out and be in full enjoyment of the premises within weeks. As though to retaliate for the chemical warfare, the groundhogs began to eat the house, noisily gnawing chunks from the woodwork. They were probably just trimming their teeth (rodent incisors grow continuously and must be actively worn down), but they had chewed through most of a back porch pillar when the occupants abandoned the house. They said they were leaving because the furnace was bad, but the fact that their latest

9

gassing had caught a skunk instead of a groundhog may have helped. Judging from the fumes that penetrated the house, the den was connected to the cellar via a drain. The house remained unoccupied.

Like the groundhog, Chestnut Ridge is at once ordinary and secretive. To the uninterested eye it just sits there, unglamorous and idle. As the groundhog is dormant below ground in cold weather, the ridge often seems quite lifeless in winter. In summer it smothers the observer in poison ivy, blackberry, honeysuckle, wild grape, and other greenery too thick to walk through, and breeds enough deerflies, mosquitoes, ticks, chiggers, and no-see-ums to completely discourage walking.

For all its prickly uncommunicativeness, the ridge is not even a quiet place. The usual American countryside din of pickup trucks, chain saws, barking dogs, and random gunfire combines with the roar of two major airports within a twenty-mile radius to make it sound like the edge of a limited-war zone. At night the network of electric light that envelopes the surrounding suburbs and roads dazzles the eyes of anyone on the ridgetop, making the woods darker than they normally would be.

Chestnut Ridge has little of the lazy expansiveness, the benign, easy flow of wilderness areas. It is a battered dwarf of wildness, a crouching, resistant groundhog of wildness with enemies too powerful and numerous to afford it much ease or generosity. On gray, still winter days the ridge woods are like the watchful, suspicious woods of fairy tales, with trees that would lay barky branches on an intruder to quell and eject him—not because they are malevolent but because the violence of human behavior toward trees has soured them. This simile is of course anthropomorphic, but the ridge's scarred slopes and battered woods cause anxieties that can inspire such phantasmagoria.

The groundhog and the ridge, though, are more than stubborn survivors. In good condition the groundhog is a handsome beast with silver-tipped fur ranging from black to blonde in color, its underparts fringed a bright rufous. When not engrossed in fattening itself for the winter, it can be lively and alert. It often climbs trees, swims like a beaver, flees from danger with headlong abandon, and will fight bravely when cornered.

Chestnut Ridge has many aspects of powerful loveliness if

some time is devoted to observing it. Indeed, the loveliness seems to increase with familiarity. The ridge can become completely alluring at times when wind, rain, mist, light, or some transient abundance of life dissolves the trammels of history and reveals its connection—broken only in the minds of human beings—with the completeness of time.

The ridge might even be said to have a soul, at least a place that is always beautiful, from which beauty radiates. There is a little grove of sugar maples on the upper west slope just below the spring-wildflower-covered mound. The maples are young, no more than sixty years old, but something about the place makes them seem venerable. They grow in an open stand without much underbrush, and the sloping expanse of gray trunks looks at once sheltered and spacious to someone entering from the brushy, gullied environs. A quiet emerald light plays on the slope in summer, and in autumn the crisp sunbeams that stream through the golden canopy make the grove sparkle like cloisonne. In winter the trees stand as gracefully against the snow as in those leafless woods through which knights hunt wild boar in a medieval book of hours. In early May a patch of dwarf larkspur blooms—a royal blue flower that grows nowhere else on the ridge.

It is certainly not an immortal soul, this maple grove. Other tree species will move in as the maples grow older. Poison ivy, Virginia creeper, or honeysuckle may cover the now uncluttered floor. The trees will die, the slope will be leveled by erosion, and the ridge will start all over again as a sandbank on some distant shore. In a sense the Chestnut Ridge described in the ensuing pages has largely ceased to exist, since most living things pass away within a year. Still, a year on the ridge is enough like other years to be the truth.

Present Time

A YEAR ON THE RIDGE

Timbrels & violins sport round the Wine Presses. The little Seed,
The sportive root, the Earthworm, the small beetle, the wise Emmet,
Dance round the Wine Presses of Luvah; the Centipede is there,
The ground Spider with many eyes, the Mole clothed in Velvet,
The earwig arm'd, the tender maggot, emblem of Immortality;
The slow slug, the grasshopper that sings & laughs & drinks;
The winter comes; he folds his slender bones without a murmur.
There is the Nettle that stings with soft down; & there
The indignant thistle whose bitterness is bred in his milk
And who lives on the contempt of his neighbor; there all the idle weeds,
That creep about the obscure places, shew their various limbs
Naked in all their beauty, dancing round the wine presses.

William Blake
The Four Zoas

SNOW COVER

I T WAS snowing on the ridge, not the damp flakes of late autumn but the hard crystals of early winter. A flock of crows that frequented the area had departed the day before, responding perhaps to some warning in the clouds. The ridge was useless to them under snow and a driving west wind.

They could find no grasshoppers and crickets in the hay meadow above the south slope, no crayfish or insect larvae in the cattail marsh and silver maple swamp at the south end, no earthworms in the leaf litter of the woods. Even the heads and entrails of butchered steers dumped by the cattle raiser who leased the hay meadow would be frozen and snow-covered. To be sure, there were poison ivy berries, dried apples and grapes, rose hips—but these were starvation foods to crows, and they knew where to find better. As with all serious crow business, their departure had been inconspicuous, quite unlike their loud clamor when they tormented owls.

With the crows gone the ridge echoed with owl calls. On this first morning of winter snow, five owls could be heard at the south end of the ridge—three great horned owls and two screech owls. They kept calling well into the dawn without interference from crows, blackbirds, or even jays. The deep hoots of the horned owls and the tremulous, descending wails of the little screech owls were the only sounds beneath the reddening sky. The horned owls were calling because their mating season was beginning, the screech owls—which had mated during the summer—for reasons known only to them.

The sun rose above the eastern hills and shone weakly for a few minutes before clouds and snow flurries obscured it. This was enough to quiet the owls, however, and a faint twitter and scolding became audible as troops of juncos, chickadees, titmice, downy woodpeckers, and nuthatches became active. A bluejay rocketed between beech branches in the south slope woods, and cardinals and towhees scratched in grapevine and poison ivy tangles. In the marsh, swamp sparrows lisped and skulked in the rice cutgrass, and a song sparrow stood on a cattail stalk and sang.

The pool below the spring that fed the marsh steamed in the freezing air: the water welling from the ridge was an even fifty-five degrees Fahrenheit, a high temperature for this morning. The marsh was frozen only on its lower reaches because of this flow of underground water, which kept up all year. A reliable source of open water during frosts, the spring had been used increasingly by wild animals since the abandonment of the house that had monopolized it. Hawks that drifted southward in winter along the interface of plateau and lowland noticed its steam and glitter. Sometimes a hawk would remain on the ridge a few days to hunt the woods and fields, but not finding abundant prey would soon drift away. The pair of red-tailed hawks that nested in the oak woods of the east slope were the only hawks the ridge supported.

Nomadic deer that crossed the ridge occasionally also used the spring. A newly shed antler still ungnawed by rodents lay on the upper reaches of the marsh. Small mammal trails wove among cattails and cutgrass, and heaps of droppings loaded with black cherry pits indicated that the marsh was a crayfish-hunting place for raccoons. Muskrat tunnels connected the bottom of the marsh with a creek that looped nearby. Parts of these tunnels were made up of clay tile that had drained the area when it had been a cornfield a decade before. The tile had become blocked, and the wetland that had been there before the first white settlers arrived had quickly reestablished itself.

The permanent spring and the marsh were touches of generosity for Chestnut Ridge. Blackhand sandstone is usually very stingy with groundwater, since its tightly cemented sand grains provide little porosity for water storage. Wells must be driven hundreds of feet to reach water tables and are likely to go dry eventually because precipitates of iron oxide clog the water veins. The well at a house on the north end of the ridge had gone dry in this way. The owners had tried pumping acid into it to dissolve the precipitates but had never gotten more than a gallon a minute afterwards, hardly enough for a shower bath. The spring water might not have originated in the Blackhand sandstone, though. There had been a lake south of the ridge after the glacier's retreat, and the spring perhaps arose from layers of gravel, sand, and peat in the silted-up lake bed. There was no easy way to determine whether this was true or not: springs are rather mysterious things. They arise like dispensations in dry and stony places and sometimes disappear abruptly, as though the places that had enjoyed them had fallen from grace. Springs are becoming much less common than they once were because ever-increasing well drilling is lowering the water tables that feed them. Whatever its origin, the spring softened Chestnut

Ridge's sandstone austerity by increasing the diversity of its life. The spring water harbored many aquatic plants and invertebrates found nowhere else on the ridge and attracted animals that would not otherwise have visited it. An occasional migrating snipe or sora rail could be flushed from the cattails, and the spring pool was a secluded resting and feeding place for mallards, wood ducks, and herons. It is surprising how quickly wild animals learn to use an amenity that becomes available—it shows how close they live to the margins of survival.

The marsh was unfrequented during the morning snowstorm. The hawks weren't flying; the deer were bedded in sheltered ravines; muskrats gnawed cattail roots in streamside dens; raccoons had taken to tree holes or moved in with hibernating groundhogs. Their dawn feeding period finished, the sparrows took cover in blackberry brambles; the only sound was a faint hissing as wind-driven snow hit the water, a sound that increased in volume through the day as the snow fell harder. The marsh became white paper scribbled over with brown cattail leaves and gray maple trunks, and the ridge almost faded from sight above it.

The white stuff from the sky seemed about to subdue the ridge, to bury its dark, coarse life under a shroud of prettiness. But the ridge had a core of life that was impervious to snow, just as the spring remained unfrozen on the coldest of mornings. Considerable burrowing and crawling went on under the frost-rimed humus and leaf litter, perhaps more than during the warm Mississippian Period before the sand became stone.

On the ridgetop near the grove of young sugar maples, a short-tailed shrew awoke from a brief but deep sleep. She had been resting from an afternoon feeding period, a feeding equally attended by the intensity that has made shrews—smallest and most primitive of placental mammals—such successful members of modern ecosystems. For shrews, the evolutionary advances of rodent incisors and grains, of ungulate molars and grass stems might as well never have occurred. They maintain an older link with the invertebrates, especially the insects. Theirs is a nutritious diet but not a dependably abundant one compared to grasses or seeds, so shrews have kept their ancestral forms and habits. Instead of growing larger or more specialized as did many other mammals, they have remained the smallest, least conspicuous, but most active and energetic of beasts. They are also among the most numerous and widespread, and their disappearance from this insect-ridden planet would have important consequences.

Sprawled in her nest of grass and leaves, the short-tailed shrew began to quiver. Her tiny eyes moved behind their lids; she was dreaming. The intense shrew dream reached its climax quickly, and she made a twittering sound, jumped up, and hurried off down one of her tunnels. Her nest was about a foot beneath the ground's surface, and it connected with a system of tunnels. Some ran as much as two feet underground, while others were just beneath the leaf litter at the surface. The shrew was hungry and moved along her dark tunnel quickly, though without the deftness of a mouse or chipmunk.

Like a mole, she was built more for burrowing than running: her strongly clawed, pink paws were bowed under her sausage-shaped body, and her gray fur was very smooth. She moved through the tightest spots without hindrance. She also resembled a mole in being somewhat larger than most shrew species. Short-tailed shrews are sometimes called mole shrews because of this resemblance. Born the previous summer, she was a full-grown individual, although not yet sexually mature.

The shrew sniffed the air in the tunnel. Her long snout looked as though it would be sharp scented but was actually rather dull, as much a burrowing tool as an olfactory organ. She smelled only the woody aroma of mold. Her small but sharp ears picked up no whisper of movement, no echo from her squeaky cries. Her long whiskers, perhaps her most effective sensing device, told her there was no food within reach. She hurried along until she reached a cache from the previous night—two small earthworms and part of a mole cricket. The crunching of her teeth on the cricket's chitinous armor was soon accompanied by a twittering of contentment.

Her teeth would have seemed terrifyingly formidable on a larger creature. Two of the lower incisors were like sabers, two of the upper like sickles. With them, she could grab and hold a tough-bodied beetle or slash a large nightcrawler to ribbons. All her teeth were tipped with a red pigment, as though living proof of "nature red in tooth and claw." She possessed another powerful weapon, one very rare for mammals: she was venomous. Some of her salivary glands produced a poison similar to cobra venom, which flowed into the wounds of her prey and slowed their respiration, making it easier for her to subdue them. Short-tailed shrews occasionally kill mice, birds, and snakes with the help of this poison, although their bite is much less effective than a snake's because they don't inject their poison as a snake does.

The earthworms and cricket didn't satiate her, but they provided her with strength to seek more substantial fare. She had not been to the surface for several days, since everything was frozen and quiet there. Now she sensed a difference in the air flowing through her tunnel and was curious. She moved toward the strangeness, and it led her upwards to a tunnel between humus and leaf litter. Small drifts of snow had sifted down through the litter; she ran through these without pausing. She had encountered snow before. The snowfalls during her short lifetime had not been more than an inch deep, however, and she was unprepared for a large pile that had drifted into a hole and completely blocked the tunnel. Sounds were strangely muffled by the snow blanket.

The shrew paused and turned away slightly in avoidance of the heaped crystals. Her whiskers picked up a few flakes, and she shook them off. A desire to investigate this change in her world was stronger than her uneasiness, though, and she began to wade toward the exit hole. Climbing up through the hole, she made a pleasurable discovery as the white powder closed over her head. She could burrow through it much more easily than through soil or leaf litter. Thrust-ing with her snout and paddling with her paws, she moved almost as quickly as she could run.

She burrowed upward, seeking the limits of this new sensation. The light increased as she climbed, and this caused neither uneasiness nor reassurance. Shrews do not mind the filtered sunlight of the forest floor, although a few minutes of direct solar radiation can be fatal. The sun was setting as the smooth snow surface sagged and fell in on her emerging head. She raised her pink snout into the windy air and a tiny puff of vapor from her breath swirled and disappeared. Above her the silhouetted sugar maples clattered brittly in the increasingly cold air.

The shrew saw very little of the landscape, only a few black cherry seedlings and aster stalks within inches of her head. Her tiny, nearsighted eyes were sensitive enough to gauge pounces on prey, but otherwise her vision was constricted and vague. She put her snout down and swam along the snow surface, leaving a winding track that was the only mark in the freshly fallen snow. There were gaps in the track when she dived and burrowed beneath the snow for a few feet, then reemerged.

Her stomach began to call—it had already digested the cricket and earthworms. The snow was enjoyable but appeared to contain no food. A horned owl hooted nearby, and a gray fox barked on the east slope. The harsh sounds startled her; shrews are extremely nervous because of their high metabolism and easily die of fright. She felt a desire for the comfortable constriction of her burrows, so she returned the way she had come until she found a hole in the leaf litter that smelled reassuringly of her own scent. Shrews have glands in their flanks that leave traces of musk as they run about, telling them where they have been and warning other shrews of their presence. She did not emerge from her burrows again that night.

The next morning the sky was clear and the wind had abated. The red-tailed hawks took to the air and had a profitable day since the snow clearly outlined the movements of rabbits, many of which were inexperienced in moving through deep snow. In the afternoon a marsh hawk skimmed over the old fields of the west slope but saw nothing of interest and kept moving south. Sunset and its owl calls came a little sooner than the previous day: the winter solstice was still a few days off.

GRAY WEATHER

The weather became warmer and remained so through the solstice. Snow melted from the south slope and from parts of the ridgetop. As the topsoil thawed and insect eggs and larvae became more accessible, the short-tailed shrew hunted closer to the surface. When the waning moon was overcast at night, she sometimes emerged to patter over the exposed leaf litter and granular, half-melted snow, searching for moth and butterfly pupae in the winter green herbs—spring avens, ground ivy, sweet cicely, kidneyleaf crowfoot, and wild blue violet.

Larger mammals were abroad in the warm spell, but the shrew's musky body was not an attraction for the self-indulgent palates of raccoons or even for the robust appetites of carrion-eating opossums. A fox or weasel might kill her in play, and an owl, with its dull sense of smell, would eat her, but she had been fortunate thus far. There would be more danger in a month or two, when the surplus of food from the previous summer was used up and the predators were eating rotten apples, which look the same after passing through the intestines of a fox or raccoon as before. Then a fox might swallow shrews.

It began to rain after the solstice. For two days the air remained warm and the rain fell in gusty squalls. The western sky boiled with gray and white clouds that turned deep pink as the sun set behind them. The western lowland took on the same greenish blue color as the backgrounds of early Flemish landscapes, and the faded leaves that still hung on the ridge trees glowed in the pink light—pale ochre of beech leaves, deep red of oak. The snow receded to shaded pockets in the quarries and north slope, and the tracks and droppings of ridge denizens increasingly marked it.

Then the days darkened, even though they were finally getting longer instead of shorter. A low ceiling of stratus clouds stretched to the horizons, the rain grew increasingly chilly, and the sunsets turned the dull red of heated iron. The long rain penetrated deep into the soil, and the dampness sapped the metabolisms of creatures underground. The short-tailed shrew shivered as she hurried along her soggy burrows, but she found enough invertebrates that had been tricked into activity by the warm spell to maintain her strength. The hawks and owls sat fluffed and morose on their perches, bereft of thermals to ride or small animal movements to watch. Even the mice were staying in their nests.

Even in this desolation there were small pockets of activity, though one had to search long to find them. In one of the brushy west slope gullies, two red squirrels chased each other around a dead American elm, making the ratchet-like chatterings of this small, feisty species. An irate Carolina wren flew at the squirrels and chased one into a hole in the elm. The other squirrel wandered off with apparent nonchalance as the wren twitched its tail a few times, then flew away.

A red-bellied woodpecker made its swooping flight up the gully and landed on the elm trunk. After glancing around for possible enemies, the gray and white bird began hitching itself up and around the dead tree, making the peevish, hiccuplike call of its species with each hop. It sounded like a gray squirrel's scolding, but there were no longer any of these common forest squirrels on Chestnut Ridge. Removal of the forest had extirpated them in the 1850s. The red-bellied woodpecker reached the top of the elm and swooped away. The rattling laugh of a pileated woodpecker sounded from the ridgetop. Then the gully lapsed into silence.

THE ARCTIC PERIOD

The dull chilly weather lasted a long time. Just when it seemed that some warmth and light could not help but return, winter hit the ridge in earnest. A storm deposited six inches of snow overnight, and the temperature dropped so low that trees began to pop with brittleness. New cracks appeared on the quarry walls as pockets of water froze and expanded. The spring steamed like a teapot, and a film of ice formed on all but the upper part of the marsh. Three small creeks draining the west slope froze, as did a fish pond where a former landowner had dammed one of them.

The weather had not been so severe at Chestnut Ridge for many years, and animals near the northern limits of their range suffered badly: bobwhite quail, Carolina wrens, red-bellied woodpeckers. If the boreal cold ended soon enough, the quail would find food and shelter in honeysuckle and poison ivy thickets and the woodpeckers and wrens would survive on wintering insects. If not, these species might be wiped out, and some might not become reestablished on the ridge for years. Such things had occurred.

As the hard freeze crept deeper into the topsoil, it cut harshly into populations that had burgeoned in preceding mild years. Amphibians and reptiles died in their sleep as cell liquids froze and sharp ice crystals pierced the cell walls, making it impossible for vital organs to function. Sometimes the organs were merely injured. The toad, snake, turtle, or salamander would awaken in spring but sicken and die later on. There were still plenty of deep, protected places, however, and none of these populations on the ridge would die out. Less mobile than the birds, they were more tenacious.

Mammals were generally better prepared than birds, reptiles, or amphibians to survive cold. If the air temperature in the burrows of groundhogs or chipmunks fell below freezing, they would wake up with a fit of shivering—an unpleasant awakening but better than none. As long as they were well fed, non-hibernating mammals could find shelter and doze through snowstorms. Shrews, moles, and mice were snug and protected beneath the thick blanket of snow. The only mammals to suffer visibly from the cold were the opossums, newcomers from the South American tropics after that continent linked up with North America about three million years ago. The tips of their naked ears and tails froze and turned black.

The snow blanket brought one additional danger to the winter-adapted mammals. A high school student who lived south of the ridge noticed the fox tracks that wove back and forth around the marsh, across the south slope, and around the cattle raiser's dumped steer heads. The snow recorded the student's interest in foxes as plainly as it revealed the foxes' interest in rabbits and mice. The tracks of a pair of brand-new, rubber-soled hunting boots obliterated or paralleled fox tracks on a wide circuit of the south ridge.

Fox furs being fashionable and prices for them high, the student hoped to make some easy money and invested in a few of the steel-jawed and wire traps that the hardware store in a near-by town carried in quantity. The steel-jawed leghold traps went onto fox trails; the wire contraptions were set at the entrances of two muskrat burrows beside the marsh. But the student appeared to know little about the life he intended to exploit, his strategy implying a belief that animals are furry mechanisms programmed to walk into traps. He seemed unaware that the traps should be boiled and concealed so the foxes wouldn't smell or see them, or that muskrats seldom used the two burrows beside the marsh. The unsprung traps gaped icily through a bitter night and a glaring, almost equally bitter day until a park agency employee found and confiscated them, probably more to the benefit of unwary local dogs than of foxes.

The moon began to wax after the snowstorm, and the nights were increasingly brightened by its reflection from the white ground. The cold made the air unusually clear, and the stars rivaled the city lights to the west. Orion vaulted above the eastern horizon. The bitter January nights had a hushed intensity that set the ridge apart from the roar of cars along the nearby county road. Owl calls seemed surprisingly loud in the hush. A barred owl—gray feathered and black eyed—loitered on the ridge a few nights and added its repertoire of barks, giggles, and shrieks to the deep, rhythmic hooting of the resident horned owls. The screech owls had stopped calling, having perhaps migrated away from the harsh conditions.

At first sight the snowy nights were like moonscapes—embodiments of frigid sterility—but there was life in them, as the owl calls indicated. Cottontail rabbits emerged from daytime shelter in drainage tiles or groundhog holes and wore dozens of paths through the brushy abandoned orchards. They dug into the snow to eat rotten apples or stretched up on their hind legs to gnaw the cambium of apple saplings. They could put these meager foods to good use because of an ingenious adaptation of rabbits. Their intestinal tracts produced special, soft fecal pellets full of protein-rich bacteria, which had digested the cellulose of the apples or bark. The pellets were nutritious and easily digestible—the rabbits ate them after excreting them. Any cellulose not assimilated in this way was excreted again as the ubiquitous, hard rabbit dropping.

This adaptation was the base of the major winter food pyramid on the ridge. With most small mammals hidden by the deep snow, the ridge would indeed have been a lunar landscape for predators if rabbits had not been able to eat their own excrement. Some rabbits died almost every night; the proteins created from apples and bark by the rabbits' symbiont bacteria could then become gray fox and great horned owl. Raccoons and opossums sniffed out half-eaten carcasses, and the red-tailed hawks soon found whatever was left in the morning.

Dawns during the arctic weather had a peculiar bloody splendor. The sun rose scarlet and flattened at each end like an overripe tomato, and sometimes an ice mist reflected the rising sun in a vertical shaft of rosy light that reached far up into a sky of pale peacock blue. At other times, streaks and smears of creek bottom fog would lattice the sunrise for a few minutes, then rush away like great dark birds as the dawn winds caught them. When the red light touched the big beeches of the south slope, the trees seemed to be on fire, their sinuous gray branches resembling swirls of smoke rising from the flames reflected on their silvery trunks.

A DEADLY CHANGE

The snow remained on Chestnut Ridge through January. A few warm days only melted the surface into a crust and compacted the rest, and more snow always fell. The short-tailed shrew grew accustomed to living under the snow. The compaction made it difficult to play in, but she established a convenient system of tunnels through the snow. She encountered a young deer mouse in one tunnel and managed to kill it—an arduous process of following the weakened mouse through the tunnel and biting it repeatedly until it finally subsided. She ate the head and breast, cached the remainder and forgot about it until several weeks later when she happened to pass the frozen carcass by accident.

Other animals also grew accustomed to finding food in the snow, and the lives of survivors became a little easier. But then another of the quick changes took place that make the adjective *temperate* seem a dubious one for the midlatitudes. As the hemisphere tilted toward the sun and warm air began to flow north from the equator, the sky turned dark and damp again. The snow began to drip in the afternoons, then froze hard in the evenings. Huge icicles formed on the quarry cliffs, but it was not good to eat them because they were laced with sulphuric acid from the polluted air of the lowland. Blood appeared on fox and rabbit trails as the melt-sharpened snow cut the feet of animals.

One day clouds boiled and scudded in chaos, and a gelid rain began to fall, freezing on contact with tree branches or weed stems. The rain continued through the night at a temperature of twenty-six degrees Fahrenheit, and in the morning there was an ice glaze on the snow thick enough for a man to walk on.

Glittering and iridescent in the morning sunlight, the glaze was among the deadliest of weather phenomena. It formed a crystal sarcophagus for several birds that had died during the night. A red-bellied woodpecker lay head down, its beak thrust into the snow. A cardinal sprawled with its neck broken from falling off its perch. A dead junco was already half eaten by an opossum, its feathers scattered. The survivors of a quail covey huddled in an ice-enameled honeysuckle thicket and made low, heartbroken sounds. The ice had made it almost impossible for them to move about, and had locked away their food supply of berries and seeds.

On the ridgetop three fox squirrels crouched on the ground. Upon emerging from their leaf nests, the big, orange-tailed squirrels had found the tree branches so ice covered as to be virtually impassable. Not as nimble at climbing as the smaller gray and red squirrels, the fox squirrels were obviously frightened and confused by the sudden treacherousness of the icy trees. Two of them huddled with their heads together as though commiserating. The other wandered about in a daze, possibly stunned from a fall. Its head would droop as though it were dozing off, then it would look up with a start and hop a few steps.

A little of the ice melted during the day, but this only made the glaze on the snow more slippery. In a west slope pasture a red fox ran up a creek bank like a tired orange dog as its claws scratched for traction on the ice. It loped wearily into the shelter of the woods, and the icy branches of the brushy woods edge clattered over its head like a bead curtain.

The temperature plunged again in the night and the ice glaze set even harder, although the evening winds freed most of the trees of their ice burdens. The bits of ice thrown off by the tossing branches tinkled and skidded merrily as they struck the ground. Creeks were encased in ice, although a trickle of water could be heard in places; but the spring on the south slope still steamed with open water.

A sharp-shinned hawk came down to drink at the spring pool the next morning, its rufous breast, slate blue back, and yellow legs and beak bright against the exhausted green of the half-frozen vegetation beside the spring. The little hawk regarded its surroundings balefully as it raised its beak to let water run down its throat. Then it circled across the pool and bulleted into the beech woods, a chilling enough sight for the chickadee or junco that would be its next meal.

A flock of robins flew over the ridge very fast, as though to keep warm. But they were flying north. Despite the abysmal conditions for worm-eating birds, their appearance signaled another change.

GROUND THAW

THE LIFE of the ridge had begun to renew itself well before the ice storm. The pair of great horned owls had begun to mate, as had the squirrels, raccoons, foxes, mink, and opossums. An eighteenth century philosophe might have been charmed at this—a beneficent Nature providing the joys of sexuality to her children during the bleakest time of year. Modern science sees more significance in a need to time reproductive activities so that the young are born when food is abundant, but there's little doubt the animals enjoyed themselves. Male raccoons and opossums came out of their tree or burrow shelters whenever the weather was bearable to search for females, the raccoons making odd whistling sounds, the opossums clicking their tongues and teeth. Fox squirrels chased one another about the ridge slopes almost every morning, although not as acrobatically as their red cousins in the gullies. Copulations were quick, almost anticlimactic, but frequent.

The ridge's invertebrate life never stopped worrying at winter's fraying shroud. Periods of frost were mere suspensions in many activities, which were quickly resumed as the temperature rose above freezing. The winter green herbs and red cedars carried on photosynthesis on warm, sunny days; and tiny yellowish springtails—insects so primitive they have no wings—underwent population explosions. Round-headed, big-eyed creatures the size of pinpoints, they hopped about propelled by switchbladelike tails and fed on algae growing in the sunlit nutrient bath of melting snow. When the temperature fell again, they had mated and left another generation of eggs.

For every springtail, dozens of brown or black oribatid mites scrambled through the dead leaves, sucking the juices of decay. They resembled eight-legged grains of silt. Tiny species of moths and flies emerged from pupal cases, mated on the snow, and left their eggs in the sheltering microclimates of bark crevices or mats of haircap moss. On particularly warm afternoons over-wintering butterflies left shelter and fluttered through the woods —purple and yellow mourning cloaks or orange brown hack-berry butterflies.

Below the frost line, where the temperature rarely fell below fifty degrees Fahrenheit, life was even less affected by winter storms. The young of some insects were intermittently active. Leathery-skinned crane fly larvae burrowed in moist ground. Orange wireworms, the larvae of click beetles, bored into roots and underground stems, and the brown nymphs of cicadas sucked the sap of tree roots. Tiny, pale centipedes, millipedes, and spiders carried on their affairs in the interstices of soil par-ticles.

Nematodes—microscopic roundworms—performed many ecological roles in the winter soil. Some infested roots, some were predators, some scavenged. They belonged to species adapted to winter conditions and would be replaced by others as the seasons changed. The smallest organisms—bacteria, fungi, and proto-zoans—thrived everywhere the soil was not frozen solid. Even the tree roots continued to absorb water. If frost were to pene-trate down the dozens of feet that many roots extended, the trees would die—not from freezing but from desiccation.

Among the few soil creatures fully inactive in winter are the earthworms, which retreat into deep underground chambers and cluster together until the thaw. Earthworms depend largely on leaf litter for food, however, so their retreat may be more from famine than from cold. The short-tailed shrew missed their activity since they were a food staple when available. This was a deprivation for her but a benefit for the ridge woods since she had to depend largely on insect larvae and pupae for food. She rushed about beneath the ridge's frozen skin like a white cor-puscle, furiously ingesting the grubs, maggots, and nymphs that could destroy its protective mantle of trees if allowed to become too numerous.

But the quiet life beneath the snow mantle was almost over for the shrew. The temperature rose above freezing for several days after the ice storm and the deathly glaze faded, but unwillingly, still refrigerating itself in shaded hollows. The smell of melting snow permeated the evening air as warm breezes blew, and snow-flattened leaf litter emerged on sunny slopes. Then rain made the small creeks run jade green above their ice. The air was full of glaucous mist, but somehow colors stood out sharply against the snow—the nose and paws of a young opossum floundering up a slushy gully were bright red, its bedraggled fur pinkish beige.

After three days of drizzle, the snow was almost gone. The thawed soil began to sag, collapsing part of the short-tailed shrew's tunnel system and smearing her with mud. She shrieked in annoyance and hurried to her nest to clean herself meticulously. That her fur retain its loft and dryness was very important. Wet, matted fur would allow the heat to escape from her body very quickly, and she would have difficulty finding enough food to regenerate it. She might die of hypothermia like an inexperienced backpacker.

The soggy, collapsing soil pressed at weak spots all over the ridge. A deep pit suddenly appeared over a culvert on the gravel township road. An unwary stroller could have fallen to the waist in it. One windy night blew down six large black cherry trees on the south slope because the soil wasn't firm enough to hold their shallow root systems. They lay the next morning with bushels of soil and sandstone clutched in their upended roots.

In the marsh a cave-in above a blocked drainage tile grew larger. Clouds of silt and sand boiled in the water that welled up in the hole. A huge blue crayfish emerged at the bottom of this turbulent pool and felt around clumsily with its pincers, frightening a much smaller reddish crayfish, which shot to the surface and took refuge on a floating twig. Both had spent winter in deep tunnels beneath the marsh. Like earthworms, crayfish are surface feeders, living mainly on decaying bits of marsh vegetation.

Everywhere on the ridge there was evidence of the soil's stirring and shifting as it thawed. So widespread and rapid were these movements, it was as though the ridge was twitching and stretching as it emerged from the snow cover, as though one stood on an awakening living being. And the soil *was* alive—it breathed, drank rainwater and snowmelt, ate dead plants and animals, and excreted them as mineralized nutrients. It was passing, on different parts of the ridge, through all the stages of life: from a thin, stony birth on abandoned quarries and ridgetop cellar holes, to a vigorous, moldy youth on the reforested slopes, to a firm, stable middle age on the level pastures and hay meadow, to an unsteady senescence on stream banks and eroded gullies.

The soil was like muscle, nerve, and fat around bedrock bone, like the thin cambium of inner bark that every year forms a new growth ring around the stony heartwood of trees. As with the ancient sandstone that underlay it, the soil was inert only to the unobserving eye, permanent only to the uncomprehending mind. It held no certainty, and failure to heed its restlessness had been the undoing of the early farmers whose cabins it had devoured. As with all living things, it was on the move ceaselessly—growing up in the interaction of dead leaves and soil organisms, falling down in the interaction of sand grains and gravity, spreading out toward reunion with its seaside origins.

The ridge soil also resembled other living things in being bounded by the year's rhythms. If it now sank and crumbled in the thaw's rivulets, it would begin to grow when the spring warmth allowed its organisms to multiply and attack the leaf litter in force. Then it would dwindle when the fall of the leaf canopy exposed it to autumnal rains, and sleep its fitful winter sleep to awaken again, perhaps stronger and fatter than during this year's thaw, perhaps not. Like all living things, the soil was vulnerable. There was always the possibility that deteriorative forces would outstrip creative, that gravity and raindrops would defeat leaf litter and microbes.

The Blackhand sandstone origin of the ridge soil made it particularly vulnerable to human disturbance. Acid sandstone soil is a good growth medium for chestnuts and oaks, but lacking calcium, a poor one for vegetables and grains. Cleared and plowed, it disintegrates unless very carefully limed and fertilized into a thin, sandy residue that will grow little except lichens and broomsedge until ash and elm seedlings begin to reclaim it. It is altogether different from the deep, black prairie soil of the Midwest, and trying to crop it is a bit like trying to raise ground-hogs for bacon.

BALMY NIGHTS

In mid-February the temperature fell and the soil surface froze again, though not as deeply as before. But the lengthening days were already triggering hormonal changes that swell the gonads of male songbirds and bring about their spring songs. On frosty mornings song sparrows were the first to start, their songs tinkling and diffident. As dawn light turned the old fields a pale cream color, tufted titmice cried "Peedle-peedle-peedle!"; cardinals whistled "Wheet! Wheet! Wheet! Wheet!"; a few overwintering field sparrows opened their pink bills and trilled "Pew! Pew! Pew! Pewpewpew-pewpew!"

In the woods bluejays made a peculiar ringing sound: "Tlapit! Tlapit!"

As the sun hit the beeches of the south slope one morning, several dozen crows trooped in from the northeast. They arranged themselves in the treetops with much swaying and flapping for balance and cawed happily. They had returned. "Kr-a-aa-a-k!" said a male crow; he left his perch and chased a smaller female over the silver maple swamp. She ducked and dodged coyly as he dived at her tail. This display of sexuality was too early for crow propriety: two other male crows sped after the amorous individual and chased him back into the trees.

Although the ground still froze at times, the deep frost was over for the year, and the life of the soil was resurgent. This was why the crows had returned. When the sun had thawed the south-facing hay meadow, the big black birds flew down and strutted across it, spearing earthworms and cutworms (the larvae of noctuid moths) that were newly active after their long winter dormancy. Cleaning soil from the worms with their feet, the crows devoured hundreds of them as well as an odd wireworm, centipede, wolf spider, and meadow mouse.

Then the weather became so balmy that even the nights were warm. The moon was new, and on the windless evenings the rustling of earthworms in the leaf litter of the wooded slopes was pervasive and distinctly eerie, as though hundreds of invisible beings were pattering about the dry leaves. The earthworms were eager to taste the newly decayed riches of last autumn's harvest. They thrust their heads from their burrows, grabbed the nearest bits of maple or ash leaf (oak leaves, full of tannic acid, are not as desirable), and pulled them underground. And they left large quantities of castings—feces—on the surface, this earthworm exchange of leaf litter and subsoil being the most important means of soil building on the ridge.

A wide range of predators took advantage of the earthworm emergence. Owls and foxes pounced on the worms; raccoons and opossums grabbed them with nimble fingers; newly emerged garter, ring-necked, and brown snakes yanked them from their burrows. The worms held on to their tunnel walls with stiff bristles, and it was sometimes easier to pull one in half than to get it all out. Woodcocks arrived from the Gulf States and fed

34

predominantly on the earthworms, using their long, prehensile (hinged at the tip) bills to pull them from the soil.

The short-tailed shrew abandoned her lower tunnels temporarily to throw herself onto the sudden abundance at the surface. She felt safe in venturing out in the dark of the moon. She caught night crawlers three times her own length, slashed them with her tusks, and, unable to eat them all, cached them away. Some of the less damaged worms revived and escaped, but she had forgotten them anyway. One pair even remained in the cache to conjugate, clinging head to tail in the mutual exchange of sperm, which insures genetic variation and natural selection in the bisexual annelids.

There seemed to be no end to the food crawling from the ridge. The shrew found moths and flies just emerging from pupal cases, their wings still soft and useless; she found large black blister beetles, their fat abdomens protruding ungracefully from under-developed wing cases, their movements slow and feeble; she found big, hairy wolf spiders in great numbers in grassy patches; she found land snails and slugs, which left shiny mucous trails across tree roots and stones. She filled her stomach in an hour, slept a few minutes, and filled it again. The increment of fats and proteins allowed her ovaries to begin the development that would shortly bring her into breeding condition.

RITES AND GAMES

In late February a warm, soft rain fell for several nights, somehow signaling to a population of spotted salamanders on the south and east slopes. The large, black amphibians with yellow-spotted backs emerged from a subterranean existence that made them virtually invisible the rest of the year and moved toward the spring pool and an oxbow pool below the marsh. (Oxbows are abandoned stream courses that become filled with rainwater.)

The male salamanders were the first to arrive at the pools. They crawled underwater, swam to the bottom, and began prowling about in an odd, stiff-legged way, lashing their tails and twining their bodies into uncomfortable-looking U shapes. Biologists call this behavior *liebspiel*—love play. As they gyrated, the males exuded into the water a sexual attractant from abdominal glands.

When the females arrived in the pools, they smelled or tasted this substance and approached the males. The excited males continued their play before the females, then pressed their cloacae against leaves and twigs, attaching to them clear, gelatinous objects about the size and shape of plastic pushpins. Inside each of these was a bead of white glandular secretion mixed with spermatozoa. The objects were spermatophores, the sperm packets that represent an intermediate evolutionary stage between the wasteful external fertilization of frogs and fishes and the chancy direct fertilization of mammals and birds. Many amphibians and most insects use them.

The jellylike objects had an attraction for the females. They crawled over the spermatophores, squatted, and picked them up with the lips of their cloacae. Inside the females the clear gel melted and the sperm emerged and was stored in crevices in the cloacal wall. As eggs descended from the ovary ducts, the sperm fertilized them. Mucus from cloacal glands covered the buckshot-size eggs, and the females laid them in packets, which they attached to underwater twigs or leaves. The packets would absorb water and expand to baseball size.

The weather began to clear and cool; somehow the spotted salamanders anticipated this. They left the pool on the last warm night just before the temperature fell. At dawn a thin film of ice covered the oxbow pool. The only evidence of the salamanders' breeding were the eggs—already somewhat camouflaged by silt and green algae—and some scattered whitish stuff resembling crumbled chalk—the leftover spermatophores. The presence of the green algae boded well for the eggs. It was a species of algae especially adapted to life on spotted salamander eggs and—perhaps by increasing the oxygen content around the eggs through its photosynthesis—it actually makes the embryos develop better. Growing in the rich nutrient bath of the egg membranes, the algae also benefit.

The day warmed, and the bright weather was a message for the ridge's chipmunk population, recently awakened, too, from its winter sleep. As the sun reached its zenith, the chipmunks emerged en masse from their inconspicuous burrow entrances under logs or stones. They were ready for *their* mating orgy, and it would be a good deal less sedate than the salamanders'.

In fact, it was downright bacchanalian. There were frenzied pursuits, squeaky shrieks of passion or rage, tail-twitching harangues delivered from atop rotten stumps. Brawling rivals tumbled down slopes, kicking and clawing at each other. This went on throughout the afternoon as dozens of male chipmunks nosed about searching for females in estrus. The females were coy and sneaky, however, sometimes giving several males the slip before letting one have his thirty-second way with her in some secluded nook.

A pair of gray foxes that denned in a brushy area of the southeast slope knew about the chipmunks' spring celebration and took good advantage of it, hunting in daylight for a change. The striped rodents were so excited that they could be approached easily. The foxes moved quietly along the slopes, dispatching and snapping up the males that blundered within pouncing distance. It was a fleeting abundance, however. The next day dawned cold and gray, the brief chipmunk estrous period was over, and the foxes went back to nighttime pursuit of the ever skinnier and less numerous cottontails. Of course, this was made easier by the fact that the cottontails were beginning their own breeding season and were often unwary. But there were no bonanzas. The female fox was carrying pups and needed all the food she could get.

The owls were nesting by this time, and the crows knew it. They watched the owls closely, especially in the early morning. Hardly a dawn went by without an explosion of caws when a roosting owl was discovered and driven from its cover in the gullies or pine plantations. The crows' excitement was uncannily similar to that of a crowd at a football game when an unexpected touchdown is made: it had the same near-hysterical quality.

The crows would chase the displaced owl, long lines of them strung out over the treetops with much flying back and forth. Finding the owl's general location for the day seemed to satisfy most of them, and they turned to the performance of aerial displays before slipping away quietly to feed. Sometimes a small group would return to vilify the owls later in the day, and another mass scolding might occur before the evening return to the

roost. If the
crows found a
chance, they would
raid the owls' nest
and throw their eggs or
owlets to the ground, but the
owl pair had managed to conceal the nest's location from them so
far. The owls knew where the crows roosted, though, and had
already captured several of them at night. A crow's intelligence
makes it hard to approach in daylight, but at night it is blind,
almost helpless, and easy prey for owls, which are thus among
the few predators really dangerous to crows. This is why crows
hate owls so much and mob them at every opportunity in daytime, when owls are—although far from blind and helpless—at
least sluggish and vulnerable.

A red-shouldered hawk wandered past the ridge during one of
these owl-mobbing mornings. This resulted in some confusion.
Nearly as large as a red-tailed hawk but with a banded tail and
red on the shoulders instead of the tail, the red-shouldered hawk
was sitting in a white oak just below the maple grove as the sun
rose. A migrating flock of grackles surrounded it, scolding the
hawk with a cacaphony of squeaking and whistling. Annoyed,
the hawk took wing. The noise ceased abruptly as the grackles
left their perches in pursuit. The whistling was replaced by

a sighing as of wind in treetops—the sound of several hundred grackle wings beating in unison.

The hawk flew across the township road, and the grackle flock veered away and left it in peace. The tranquility was short-lived, however. Two crows on their way to the owl mobbing spotted the hawk as it rose above the trees and dived after it. By happenstance the hawk fled toward the gully where the owl was being persecuted. On arrival there, the two crows were confused, suddenly being confronted with two victims instead of one. They perched in a tulip tree to consider this embarrassment of riches while the hawk alighted in a red oak across the gully and then watched as the crow flock cawed and dived at the big owl.

Evidently this activity appealed to the red-shouldered hawk for it left the oak and made a pass at the owl, shrieking like the rustiest of iron gates in its excitement. The owl, petulantly ensconced in a white pine, paid no attention to its new persecutor, and the crows were too excited about the owl to bother with the hawk. Joining the attack on the owl was actually a good way of diverting the crows' attention from itself, but it's doubtful the hawk did so on purpose: hawks are not very intelligent.

The hawk circled screaming around the owl several more times, then dived into the woods, where it landed in a tree and looked back as though perplexed by the whole affair. When the owl at last broke cover and the crows voiced an ecstatic outburst of caws, however, the hawk circled the gully again, its wings taut and quivering with excitement. But the owl merely flew quietly away through the pine planatation in search of another roost.

Thoroughly aroused, the hawk flew to the ridgetop and stalked a rabbit in a poison ivy thicket, until the rabbit was frightened away by a pair of dogs chasing a groundhog. The dogs harried the groundhog into a clump of multiflora and nosed around it patiently, waiting for the rodent to venture out. The hawk gave up on this confusing round of attacks and continued its northward migration.

THE FINAL SNOWFALL

The weather warmed again at the beginning of March, and the increasingly long twilights took on an extraordinary softness.

The leafless woods receded into distances that seemed faraway and slightly melancholy, while warm breezes full of the sweetness of greening grass moved across the pastures. Around the marsh the silver maple flowers burst their buds—thousands of unpetaled clusters, some with bright red pistils, some with yellow stamens, some with a few of both. The grasslike leaves and pink flower buds of spring beauty appeared on the south slope, and a golden haze of slippery elm flowers spread over the brush tangles of the west slope.

As dusk faded into night, these brushy places generated peculiar sounds: first a series of nasal squawks, then a protracted whistling that ended abruptly in a twittering and soft roaring. After a silent interval, the squawks would start again and the whole sequence would be repeated. Sometimes the squawking came from one location while whistling and twittering went on in another.

Male woodcocks made these sounds as they performed their mating display, sometimes with females watching, sometimes without. The squawks were their calls as they strutted about small glades with tails spread and breast feathers puffed up. Sometimes they tripped over goldenrod stems in their excitement. The whistling was the sound of their wings as they took off and circled high into the gloaming, while the twittering and roaring were respectively vocal and wing sounds as the birds dived headlong back to their strutting ground.

As the new moon waxed and grew brighter, the woodcock raptures went on well into the night. Amorous male groundhogs left their homes and crept about the quarries searching for the burrows of females. Unlike the chipmunks, they were phlegmatic about mating. There were few fights between rivals. Groundhogs often climbed trees to eat the buds at this lean time.

The short-tailed shrew responded to the changes in the air. Her ovaries matured and began to produce egg cells, and the scent-producing glands on her flanks that usually marked her tunnels dried up. At other times the scent served as a repellent to other shrews: in its absence male shrews could respond to the attraction of her estrous state without fear.

Several males lived in the vicinity. Driven by their own swelling testes, they soon found her. With much twittering and nimble, if short-sighted, pursuit, they courted her, and all won her at one time or another. Shrew ovaries are sluggish, and the upheavals of repeated copulation are needed to shake the egg cells loose from the ovary walls. Finally five egg cells descended the Fallopian tubes and met the spermatozoa of the various males. The fertilized ova then attached themselves to the uterine walls and began to multiply and grow at a fast, shrewlike pace.

The prospective mother became hungry and irascible, and the males abandoned her in favor of another female that had just come into estrus. The prospective mother was somewhat worn out by their attentions anyway and welcomed a return to her normal, frenetic pursuit of food, a pursuit made more difficult by the changes in her body.

Winter interrupted the thaw once more. Thunderstorms broke up the soft weather as a front of cold air moved in and forced the warm air upwards into cumulonimbus clouds. At one moment the evening was quite still—the air a little heavy, with a rosy gray light—then a clap of thunder sounded, the sky darkened abruptly, and a heavy rain thumped down. Undeflected by foliage, the rain flooded the earthworms' burrows and drove the short-tailed shrew out of the less well-drained parts of her tunnel system. Earthworms came to the surface in great numbers as the flooding exhausted the oxygen in their burrows, and predators took advantage of this after the rain had stopped. By morning, ground that had been littered with worms was once more clear of them, the survivors having reentered the burrows.

After the thunderstorms, the evening was cold again and the earthworms stayed underground. The sky broke up into chilled fragments of a transparent, almost colorless blue, and opaque clouds piled up above the western horizon. As the sun set, shafts of platinum light slanted northward and the sky turned a faint salmon color below the gray cloud layer.

It snowed the next chilly morning, big flakes that quickly whitened the ground. In the swamp, festoons of snow lay on silver maple flowers that had already set fruit—small, fuzzy samaras like yellow green mouse ears. On the upper slopes the snow temporarily buried some spring beauty blossoms and the newly emerged leaves of fawn lily and cutleaf toothwort.

WOODLAND FLOWERS

HIGH winds from the southwest grasped the ridge and soon evaporated the last snowfall. They shook the unfolding flowers of box elder and willow, and invisible clouds of pollen flew northeast. The winds seemed to awaken the spring wildflowers: as they burst from the ridge they seemed more like colorful, sessile little animals than plants. Masses of spring beauty nodded and tossed in the woods or under pasture trees. Bloodroot came up with its gray green leaves folded around spindly white petals, which the wind would blow away a few days after the flowers opened. The purplish foliage and cross-shaped flowers of cutleaf toothwort covered most wooded places. Little patches of rue anemones appeared in the least disturbed parts of the woods. The low-lying, pink or white rue anemone blossoms seemed ephemeral, but they would persist on their wiry stems after the wind had blown other early wildflowers to pieces.

Wildflower populations on Chestnut Ridge were not very abundant or diverse. The soil was unsuitable for the more specialized species of either lowland or plateau, and any rare species that might have been there had been removed by a century of disturbance. Only common species that could survive grazing, logging, and general trampling remained.

The same was true for the other major indicator of spring in the eastern deciduous forest—the frogs. Two hundred years before, the wetland below the spring probably was the breeding place of large populations of spring peepers, striped chorus frogs, and wood frogs. A visitor to the ridge then would have experienced a din that disorders the senses. A chorus of the males of these three species might be compared to a tape recording of a room full of enthusiastic but insane sopranos and basso profundos, a recording played at full volume and at a faster speed than the one at which it was recorded.

"Eeeeeeeeeeeeeeeeeeeee! Preeeeeeeeeeeeeeeeeeeee! Squeeeee-eeeeeeeeek" the sopranos screech, while the bassos grunt, snort, and shout nonsense like "Rubber Ducky! Rip a Zipper! Rub a Dub Dub!" The sopranos are the spring peepers and chorus frogs, both tiny species that sing by inflating balloonlike throat sacs. They appear in thousands to sit in the water at the edge of swamp pools. The bassos are the wood frogs, brown, forest-dwelling relatives of the common leopard frog. They make their grunting calls with voice sacs on each side of the throat. Never as numerous as the peepers and chorus frogs, they compensate with sheer volume as they kick their way about the swamp pools in search of females.

The ears literally ring for hours after listening close-up to such a chorus, but there had not been one at Chestnut Ridge within memory. Not enough habitat remained. A few chorus frogs swelled their orange throats in pools among the cattails. A few peepers swelled their white and brown-speckled ones in pools under the silver maples. But there were no longer any wood frogs on the ridge, since the species thrives only in fairly large areas of moist woodland.

The ridge did boast splashes of abundance, however. A swarm of fairy shrimp appeared in the oxbow pool where the salamanders had bred, obscuring the amphibians' eggs with their multitudes. Fairy shrimp are inch-long crustaceans endemic to woodland pools that flood in winter and dry up in summer. The shrimp hatch, pass through a larval stage, breed, lay eggs, and die between the fall rains and the drying of their pool. Sometimes they do not appear at all in pools where they were abundant a year before. The transience and unpredictability of their lives perhaps account for their abundance, since no predator can depend on them.

At first glance the fairy shrimp resembled swarms of tropical fish—their narrow, tapered bodies were very colorful. They had red tail bristles, orange tails marked with blue stripes of intestine, reddish ochre legs and abdomens, orange heads, and blue black eyes. Many carried turquoise blue egg sacs at their midsections—the tiny eggs were visible—and a few carried larger sacs, which had turned yellow. They swam upside down, with undulating motions of their multiple legs. Every square inch of the pool seemed to contain at least one fairy shrimp.

The oxbow pool was alternately a mirror and an aquarium as the March winds drove clouds overhead. When the clouds hid the sun and ruffled the water, the pool appeared silvery and opaque, barred with the black of reflected sycamores and maples. When the sun came out again, the warm light pierced the water and revealed the fairy shrimp's bright colors, the orange and black of water boatmen, the scarlet of water mites, the yellow of fishfly larvae, and the black, green, ochre, and sienna of fallen leaves at the bottom. It was hypnotic to look into the sunlit pool, and then it became fantastic as a pattern of fallen leaves suddenly came to life and crawled along the bottom. A two-foot snapping turtle from the creek had taken up residence in the oxbow, presumably to eat fairy shrimp. Its lumpy legs and carapace camouflaged it perfectly when it wasn't moving.

The turtle swam to the pool's surface, resting with only its eyes and snout above the water. A cloud went over, and the turtle's head, protruding from the suddenly opaque surface, resembled a stick until its eyes blinked and it swam a few inches. There appeared to be no enemies about, and the air was pleasantly warm, so the turtle crawled onto a fallen log and fell asleep, becoming so still that it might have been dead.

The snapping turtle had appeared mysterious and rather beautiful in the water. In the full light, however, its pinkish rolls of flesh, knobby tail, and almost shapeless head made it seem incomplete, as though its existence only imperfectly bridged the gap between life's organization and the random arrangement of stones and leaves on the pool's bottom. But when a plane flew low overhead and the turtle opened its eyes, there was no doubt as to its vitality. One could imagine a pair of glittering black eyes suddenly appearing on a stone gargoyle.

NEW ARRIVALS

As the vernal equinox approached, the southwest wind brought a flight of male red-winged blackbirds to the ridge. They quickly dispersed to carve out breeding territories in the marsh and hay meadow, chasing one another from treetop to treetop in the silver maples and incessantly crying "Pope Leo! Pope Leee-o!" in their bubbling, squeaky voices. Small flocks of robins appeared and sat swaying in clumps of honey locust and sassafras saplings. They sang with such cheerful mindlessness that their three-syllable phrases might have been "Oh well! What the hell! What, me worry?"

The warm wind enticed more of the zoomorphic little plants from the ridge. Leaf-wrapped stems of mayapple popped up in the woods. Most had shiny, round flower buds on their tops, and they grew in colonies, so they looked like troops of green-helmeted gnomes. In the silver maple swamp and other damp, shaded places, the two-leaved sprouts of jewelweed dotted the leaf litter like resting flights of jade green butterflies.

The wind usually blew throughout the days, but sometimes it stopped for a while just before sunset. Then the crows did somersaults and loop-the-loops on their way back to the roost, and turkey vultures—newly arrived from Kentucky—glided over the ridge in a silence intensified by the distant roar of automobiles and jetliners. The last rays of the sun shone brightly on their redskinned heads.

After the sun went down, the wind rose again, shaking the treetops with a writhing and clattering quite different from the swaying and rustling of wind in leafy trees. Birds fled from this turbulence, and the trees were often the only things moving in the twilight. Sometimes, however, the gusts descended to the ground and threw up bunches of dead leaves in the manner of excited apes.

The wind was an aspect of Chestnut Ridge that impressed itself almost subliminally upon the observer. At first it seemed unrelated to the ridge, an alien force that operated mechanically, but one gradually came to realize that all perceptions of the ridge were influenced by the wind. The movements it gave to trees, grasses, leaves, and clouds were as important as the colors and shapes that sunlight gave to them. The wind came to have a power over the imagination that was a direct function of its lack of substantiality. Having no form, always changing, it passed through the mind like a recurring doubt, scattering conclusions about the nature of things as it scattered fallen leaves.

If the soil was the flesh of the ridge, the wind was its breath—the sometimes faint but always present susurrus that proved its life. That the wind originated not in the sandstone but at the equator did not make it less a part of Chestnut Ridge. Like breath, it brought the freshness the ridge woods needed and carried away their foulness. It brought pollen to fertilize flowers, migrating birds to protect them from insects, summer storms so their fruits wouldn't wither. If the wind had died permanently, the ridge would have suffocated.

Of course, such analogies can only be carried so far. If the wind brought breath to the trees, it also blew them down from time to time. It was often an erosive force, sometimes a frightening one, as when it rose suddenly in the woods and tossed trees weighing tons as easily as it tossed the hay meadow grasses. But even its violence could lift the heart. It drove ponderous cumulus clouds overhead so swiftly that their shadows slid across the sunny ridgetop like galleons cresting a wave. In the end the wind was the definitive element of wildness on the ridge, the force that linked it most powerfully—more powerfully than bedrock—to its primeval origins. The wind seemed to carry a fragrance of forests never felled, of prairies never plowed—as though it still circulated the breath of every passenger pigeon and bison that ever lived (as indeed it does). Whether it caressed or abraded, the wind always expressed the multitudinous, anarchic will of the biosphere, a will that makes itself known not in commandments but in the passage of eons.

On the
south slope
the wind in the
old hollow beeches
caused some anxiety
for a raccoon. She
peered from a hole far
up in one of these trees
as the tree swayed and
creaked. Beech wood is
brittle, and there are
often huge branches or
whole tops of beeches
on the ground after a windstorm. The
raccoon made as if to crawl out of the hole,
putting first her front end, then her rear end,
then her front end again out of the cavity. Finally only her tail was visible, then that disappeared back into the tree also. A moment later
she appeared again, peering anxiously from a
small hole about twenty feet lower. She had several
newborn young in the tree and was apprehensive about leaving
them in order to seek food.

After dark the rustling of earthworms in leaf litter was still
audible, although wind noises concealed it somewhat. Otherwise
the wind inhibited animal movements. The short-tailed shrew
did not like to come out in wind because it disturbed her hearing. Insects were hard to find on windy nights anyway. Newly
emerged moths—codling moths resembling bits of bark or lichen
and large maple spanworm moths with brown wings mimicking
dead leaves—clung to tree trunks instead of fluttering through
the woods in search of mates.

The vernal equinox arrived with thunderstorms and chilly
rains, and the spring unfolding came to a standstill for several
days. No new flowers or leaves appeared. Half-opened buds of
buckeye or mayapple stopped unfurling as if caught in some
guilty act. Songbirds that had been overwintering in the marsh
continued to do so, although they were increasingly territorial as
their nesting instinct asserted itself. A swamp sparrow and a

female cardinal chased each other about in the cattails, while two male cardinals performed threat displays at each other in the silver maples. The cardinals fled, and the sparrow threw back its head and sang the faint, lispy trill of its species. Besides the jewelweed seedlings, the only sign of spring at the marsh was a blossoming mazzard cherry above the spring pool. Its cloud of white blossoms looked tentative and unconvincing against the gray sky.

But things began to happen very quickly when the next warm spell came. A colony of daffodils appeared almost overnight in a blackberry patch on the west slope, a relic of some forgotten cabin garden. Redbuds blossomed in gullies where glacial till and limestone, washed down from the township road, provided the alkaline soil conditions upon which this magenta-flowered little tree thrives. On the east slope the sweet fragrance of tiny golden spicebush flowers filled the moist woods. A colony of large-flowered trillium came up on the north slope, the three leaves and flower bud of each plant crumpled and fisted to break through the leaf litter. Sometimes a trillium would come up through a hole in a large dead leaf: as though caught in a snare, the plant would be unable to unfold and would wither away.

Violets began to blossom everywhere—common blue violets, smooth yellow violets, and white pale violets. They carpeted the ground in the brushy second growth woods. Other winter green plants such as crowfoot, cicely, and avens had taken good advantage of their photosynthetic head start. Some of them had put out new leaves and stems a foot tall already. This early growth was a necessity for these woodland herbs, since the vast leaf surface of the tree canopy would soon monopolize most of the soil moisture and sunlight.

The sugar maple buds burst open and the green gold haze of their flowers spread across the ridgetop, making spring visible from a distance. The slippery elm fruits were almost mature, bright yellow wafers on otherwise bare branches, and their leaf buds had begun to swell. Apple and pear trees in the abandoned orchards blossomed profusely, and the abundant insect and songbird populations that frequent unsprayed fruit trees materialized instantly—a crowded buzzing of honeybees, bumblebees, iridescent halictid bees and syrphid flies; yellow and red crab spiders and tortoise beetles with golden shells; an excited fluttering of golden- and ruby-crowned kinglets, yellow-rumped warblers, blue gray gnatcatchers, and eastern phoebes.

Crows began to spend a lot of time loitering in pine plantations, good nesting places for these secretive birds. Crows and jays are so adept at concealing their nests that comparatively little is known about their mating habits. The male crows sang every morning—rattling sounds that sometimes ended in cooing notes. Females cried "Car! Car!" and made begging motions as males sidled up to them, bowing and scraping, their feathers puffed up to make them look fine and impressive. Sometimes a crow pair would sit together for hours, picking tenderly with their bills at each others' head feathers. Male grackles also used the puffed feather method of attracting females, looking rather like animated feather dusters as they strutted before prospective mates in west slope pastures. The females did look distinctly awed by this.

Among the most persistent sexual solicitors of the ridge were the rufous-sided towhee males. The brightly marked, white, black, and orange birds skulked inconspicuously in the brush for most of the year, but now they stood boldly atop shrubs and saplings and sang most of the day. Each bird sang a personal variant of the northeastern race of towhee's mating phrase, which is usually transcribed as "Drink your *tea!*" A male beside the hay meadow sang "Drink *tea!*"; another on the west slope sang "Drink *your* tea!"; yet another just outside the maple grove sang "*Your* tea!" It was unclear what the females made of all this variation, but some males seemed to attract more females than others.

APRIL HEAT

The short-tailed shrew did not even remember the thrills of her courting period. She had been moving about with increasing hunger and discomfort as the fetuses in her uterus grew, and her three-week pregnancy was made even more arduous by a need to clean out and enlarge her nest. She had no idea why she was performing all this labor, and the precision of her response to a completely unknown situation remains one of the everyday mysteries that make such questions as the origin of the solar system seem almost simple by comparison.

Late one night the shrew crawled panting back to her nest and unloaded her burden. She licked each infant as it emerged from her vagina, removing the amniotic sac, which she immediately ate. Three of the blind, naked, and toothless infant shrews struggled and gasped as they felt the roughness of her tongue and the chill of the air. She allowed these to crawl to her six teats, now full of milk. The other two didn't move, they were defective and stillborn—a condition perhaps related to the poisons still bound up in the ridge's soil from former orchard operations. The shrew ate the dead infants along with the afterbirths.

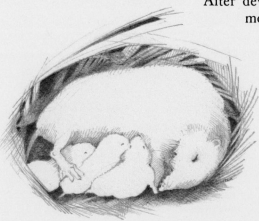

After devouring everything not moving in the nest, she crouched quietly and cleaned herself while the infants sucked until their bellies were round and hard. If there had been light in the nest, the infants' internal organs would have been visible through their skins.

Their long snouts and pink, almost shapeless bodies made them look absurdly like paunchy, humanoid cartoon characters. Their sucking felt good to the shrew after the pain of their births. Her stomach was full. She twittered drowsily. When her offspring stopped feeding, she curled around them and went to sleep.

The next day dawned clear and warm, so warm that the shrew found her upper burrows uncomfortable when she left her nest to seek food. She followed a newly dug mole tunnel down to cooler temperatures. Suddenly she paused with her nose raised and listened. Faint stirring sounds came from the tunnel wall—perhaps it was a beetle grub. But the sounds increased and the wall began to bulge. Bits of earth fell from the ceiling. The shrew became frightened and hurried back the way she had come. It was just in time because the tunnel suddenly collapsed and a large, scaly claw protruded into it.

The claw paused a moment, then stirred again, churning loose earth, sandstone pebbles, twigs, and bits of dead leaf as it pushed its owner, an old box turtle, upward. The mole tunnel had passed close by the turtle's hibernaculum in an abandoned groundhog burrow, and the turtle was coming out to enjoy the warmth of the day. It was not the first time he had emerged that spring; the warm weather in March had brought him out also, but this venture was the earliest in the morning.

At the surface a slight depression in the leaf litter was the only sign of his nighttime refuge. It stirred slowly and rustled as the solemn head of the turtle emerged. Although the irises of his eyes were bright red, a trait of most male box turtles, he was inconspicuous. The orange markings on his dark gray head and carapace were a deceptively showy coloration, since they blended so well with the leaf litter as to make him almost invisible when not in motion.

The turtle rested at his refuge entrance most of the morning. The warmth and the bright colors of the sunlit woodland perhaps pleased him. He had little if any recollection of other emergences into sunlight, but there had been many. He was the oldest animal on the ridge. He had been twenty years old before he reached his full six-inch length and had survived uncounted years since then. Box turtles have been known to live over half a century in the wild if they have the good fortune not to be run over by an automobile or killed by an untimely frost. The old turtle had probably been around longer than most of the humans in the vicinity.

By noon it had become too hot on the ridgetop, and the turtle moved into a west slope gully, pausing along the way to eat elm samaras brought down by the wind. The leafless woods were rather parched in the heat: the bloodroot, toothwort, and fawn lilies that the turtle passed had already dropped their blossoms. Others had appeared to replace them. Kidneyleaf crowfoot bore blossoms resembling miniature buttercups (they belong to the same genus). Wild blue phlox opened five-petaled blossoms among the rocks of the Woodlander mound, and pink-flowered wild geranium had appeared among the north slope trilliums.

The box turtle wandered to the bottom of the gully and rested on the cool sand of a creek bed through the afternoon. It was a very still day. Only butterflies seemed active. Swallowtails, red admirals, falcate orange tips, and silver-spotted skippers fluttered about or landed on the creek mud to suck moisture from it. Small blues and dark brown elfins rested on the mud in clusters that resembled strange blossoms. The old turtle blinked at the butterflies and ate a few slugs and land snails. When it got too warm, he crawled into a puddle.

When the gully fell into shadow, the turtle began climbing back to the ridgetop. Currents of cooling air were trickling downhill, and he would be in danger if caught in a frost pocket, some low place that filled up with below-freezing air even when ridgetop temperatures remained over fifty degrees Fahrenheit. He was back in his refuge by the time a full moon began to silver the maple trunks and mayapple leaves. The dryness and dropping temperature inhibited earthworms, so there was not much rustling in the leaf litter; and the squeaking of bats and whistling of night migrating birds were audible above the treetops.

A less audible but equally intense seasonal activity was taking place in the treetops themselves. Maple, oak, and beech flowers had been wind-pollinated in the warmth of the day, and the pollen grains that adhered to the stigmas were growing their pollen tubes down the styles toward the ovaries. Some had already penetrated and fertilized the ova, and the cells were dividing and forming embryos. To support this activity—so tiny in individual manifestation but vast in concert—a massive fountain of sap and hormones surged up the xylem of the trees' bark from the root networks, and the roots pulled ceaselessly at water and dissolved nutrients in the soil. It was a great tax on the soil's fertility, and what was creative for the trees might have been destructive for the soil had not the fallen leaves and branches been returned to it in the end.

A small white-tailed deer herd moved onto the moonlit ridge, following an aisle of woodland along the creek below the marsh. There were three old does and a young doe and buck—both yearlings. Two of the does were pregnant and uneasily in search of a quiet expanse of food and cover in which to bear the fawns.

They traversed the ridgetop, but it seemed too exposed, too beset with city lights, traffic noise, and airplane roaring. They kept moving west and crossed the township road into the heavy brush and pastures. They smelled the white-faced Herefords, which the cattle raiser had just released in the pastures, and the smell attracted them. They jumped the pasture fence and began to crop the grass, looking elfin beside the clumsy bulk of the cattle.

AN EARTHWORM ODYSSEY

The next day was as hot and still as the last, and a lassitude settled on the ridge. The trill of American toads from a fishpond on the west slope was the only sound for most of the afternoon. "Dreeeeeeeeeeeeeeeeeeeeeeeeeeeeemmmmmmm." It was like a sweet buzzing in the ears during some half-pleasurable fever delirium. Toads produce their lazy, sensual call by inflating a throat sac in the manner of peepers and chorus frogs, but it is a much subtler song despite the toads' larger size. The males sat in the water with their heads and shoulders showing like portly bathers at a sedate resort. When a female approached, the nearest male clambered on her back and grasped her flanks hard with his front feet. This encouraged her to extrude long strings of eggs, over which the male ejaculated clouds of sperm. Sometimes males clambered on the backs of other males but were soon discouraged by indignant squeaks.

The ridge's other resident frog species, the green frog, had begun to call beside the little creeks that meandered through the west slope pastures. Resembling scaled-down bullfrogs, the greens were at once the largest and most timid of the local frogs. They lacked the protection of the toad's nasty tasting skin and the peeper's and chorus frog's smallness. Although there were many in the lush grass beside the creeks, one rarely saw a green frog. Usually the only indications of their presence were a squeak and a plop as a frog gave its alarm call and hopped into the water.

Green frog calls were probably the loudest on the ridge—an explosive "Tonk!" that sounded like a snapped banjo string—but the timid creatures almost always sang alone and at scattered intervals. They seldom produced a raucous chorus like the wood frogs', and one never saw a green frog calling in the ridge pastures. They slipped quietly out of sight at the first suspicious movement.

On this hot day a green frog that had been calling beside a sandy bank took alarm at a movement in the grass. He swam to the other side of a shady pool, startling a school of redbelly dace (a kind of minnow) that had been loitering there. The rustling and heaving in a sandy tuft of grass might have been a common water snake, arch enemy of green frogs. But no snake appeared and the heaving stopped. The striped minnows went back to watching the pool's surface for floating insects, and the frog hopped downstream in search of more tranquil surroundings.

The rustling in the grass started again, louder than before, and eight earthworms suddenly emerged from the heaving soil as though squeezed from toothpaste tubes. Seven of the earthworms emerged in entirety and crawled away in various directions, but the eighth suddenly reversed direction and disappeared backward into the soil, from which barely audible smacking sounds began to come. An eastern mole that had been pursuing the earthworms had grabbed it, pulled it back into its tunnel, and was now eating it.

The seven surviving worms showed a surprising degree of individuality in response to this sudden eviction. The three largest and brownest worms moved a little way through the grass and burrowed back into the soil as though accustomed to escaping from moles. The other four began crawling across the sandy bank toward the creek pool, which seemed an unpromising direction. Desiccation and solar radiation can kill earthworms very quickly.

The two larger and browner worms reached the water quickly, put their heads in, recoiled, and set out crawling along the edge of the pool. One crawled upstream, the other downstream. Both soon reached grassy patches of ground into which they too burrowed. The other two worms, the smallest and pinkest, clearly had difficulty crossing the sunlit sand. They crawled a little way, curled up in discomfort at the burning rays, then crawled a little further.

The larger of the two reached the water first. It put its head in and recoiled, but instead of setting off along the pool's edge, it put its head back into the water as a skittish bather might dip his foot back into water that wasn't *too* cold. After some hesitation, this explorer worm entered the water completely and began crawling across the bottom, actually making better progress than on the bank.

It had crawled about halfway across the pool when one of the dace noticed it. The minnow grabbed the worm by the head and swallowed about two-thirds of it before the other dace became aware of their schoolmate's good fortune and began to chase him around the pool. Since the worm was as long as the dace, this almost instantaneous swallowing (as though a man were to devour in one gulp a salami four feet long) was impressive. Furthermore, the dace managed to ingest the remaining third of the worm while being pursued hotly by his companions. Even after that, they kept following him around as though he must have a secret worm supply.

Meanwhile, the smallest, pinkest worm had come only about halfway across the sand bank and appeared exhausted. It stopped moving forward and began writhing about feverishly. The sand grains that had stuck to its mucous sheath were insufficient to shield it from the deadly solar radiation. Soon it would be a dark brown worm mummy.

Suddenly a robin fluttered down and grabbed the worm and would have eaten it on the spot if not for the sand grains. Instead it ran into the grass to clean the worm, and a starling flying toward the cattle herd spied the worm. It swooped at the robin and the startled bird dropped its catch. But the robin had a nest nearby and was feeling aggressive. Recovering from its surprise, it charged the starling and chased it away. The worm sank into the grass, forgotten and safe for the time being.

THE CANOPY UNFOLDS

Cattail shoots came up in the marsh, resembling green flames among the previous year's dry leaves. Jewelweed seedlings reached ankle height and silver maple leaves unfolded. Swamp sparrows, white-throated sparrows, and juncos that had spent the winter around the marsh went north to nest and were replaced by red-winged blackbirds. The brown-feathered female red-wings arrived—several weeks after their red- and yellow-chevroned male counterparts—and began weaving nests in cattails and meadow grasses.

The all-year spring kept the marsh wet in the hot weather, but the water level in the oxbow pool was already much lowered. Masses of filamentous green algae congealed the water, suspending the corpses of numerous fairy shrimp. A few of the shrimp still swam about in patches of open water, but their season was almost over. The spotted salamander egg masses were collapsed ruins: the bushy-gilled larvae had hatched and now lurked in the pool shallows.

The snapping turtle had gone back to its permanent home in the creek.

The woodland flowering reached its peak during these still, sunny days of early May. Large-flowered trillium blossoms dotting the north slope resembled myriads of white eyes peering from the shade. The showy blossoms turned pink at their petal bases as seeds grew in their ovaries. Golden ragwort, a springtime relative of the late summer sunflowers and goldenrods, added its brilliant yellow flower heads to the softer pink and violet of wild geranium and blue phlox.

Tree flowers were less conspicuous but far more numerous than herb flowers. The pawpaw trees among the trilliums bore bell-shaped, maroon flowers that looked artificial hanging from the bare branches. In brushy places sassafras trees put out fragrant golden flowers shaped like tiny stars. Little bee-mimic flies visited them in great numbers to sop nectar from glands between the petals. The yellow, red, or purple stamen and pistil clusters of wind-pollinated trees were the most numerous flowers but were hard to distinguish from the unfolding leaves, which also were yellow, red, or purple when they burst their buds. Only after a day or two in sunlight did they assume the tender green foliage of May.

The new leaves and flowers had begun to wilt in the sultry weather when a violent thunderstorm broke the heat. Its strong winds and heavy rains brought down a large black cherry weakened by carpenter ants and littered the woodland floor with racemes, bud scales, leaf bracts, and other detritus of the trees' awakening. The storm heralded a cold front, which moved in the next day; temperatures fell below freezing that night. Leaves of ash, hickory, and pawpaw blackened and shriveled. Oak and maple leaves merely curled up, expanding again unharmed when the temperature rose the following morning.

Soaked earth and lowered temperatures brought forth another flowering of sorts. On underground mats of fungus mycelia, buttonlike growths formed and developed with amazing swiftness, bursting through the leaf litter as elongate, wrinkled morels. Middle-aged men came from miles around to fill sacks with these delicious mushrooms and with the wild leeks that grew near them. In true Appalachian fashion the mushroom and leek pickers also kept an eye out for ginseng, but they never found any. It was another of the ridge's vanished amenities.

Another valuable crop grew on the ridge at this time, but the mushroom pickers were unaware of it. A grassy place on the south ridgetop contained a patch of feral asparagus, all that remained of a vanished house's vegetable garden. The spears of asparagus were scattered through the tall grass, virtually invisible unless one stood still a moment and let the eyes focus. Once spotted, though, the thick sprouts seemed to leap from the grass. A half hour's careful search would locate enough sprouts for several meals, but there were always a few more hiding in the grass. A month later the asparagus patch would be advertised blatantly by tall, feathery mature stalks, but by then the forager would have lost his chance for that year.

The cool weather did not retard the growth of new leaves very much. A thin but noticeable forest canopy unfolded over the ridge within a few days. The short-tailed shrew found the unaccustomed shadiness helpful since it made easier her hunt for the insects that were emerging from newly green tangles of poison ivy, Virginia creeper, black cherry seedlings, and false Solomon's seal.

Since her infants had already doubled in size, she needed all the food she could get. Clothed in short pelts of brownish gray fur, the young shrews were still weak and unsteady, tottering about the nest with heavy-headed clumsiness, but they were strong enough to attack their mother's teats purposively and vocally. The nursing process was becoming less pleasurable to her because of this increasingly boisterous behavior, so she spent less time in the nest.

There was much to interest her outside. Large numbers of fat, brown May beetles emerged from the ground and bumbled about noisily in the underbrush before taking wing in search of mates. They were easy for the shrew to capture, as were click beetles, adults of the wireworms she had hunted in the soil during the winter. The insects were sluggish during the cool nights, and the shrew could catch moths that had emerged from pupae on the ground and were unable to fly because of the chill. Hunting would become harder for her as the nights grew warmer and the leaves enlarged, because much of the burgeoning life of the ridge would climb into the treetops, where she could not follow.

The wildflowers beneath the canopy surrendered even before its shade was complete. Trilliums and wild geraniums lost their petals and grew ragged and brown around their edges. Toothwort and spring beauty faded into crispy mats of withered stems. The woodlands began to take on the drab colors of summer— green of treetops, brown of leaf litter. Rue anemone persisted in places, however, and dwarf larkspur blossomed in the maple grove, its blue flowers spots of brilliance in already deep shade.

BIRD SONGS

PLANT growth spurted in the hay meadow and marsh as it slowed in the unfolding woodland shade. Blackberry vines blossomed on the ridgetop, jewelweed was shin-high in wet places, and the meadow was full of red clover and yellow rocket, a species of mustard. The female red-winged blackbirds boldly defended their nests in cattails and meadow grasses, nests that were anyway almost impossible to locate in the dense herbage. Four groundhogs that had established burrows in the hay meadow seemed hardly to know what to do with the wealth of plant life: the tousled masses of leaves and stems around their holes suggested that they couldn't eat the plants fast enough to keep the meadow at bay.

The weather became brilliant and breezy, and the thigh-high grasses and forbs of the hay meadow waved and rippled with prairielike freshness and expansiveness, even though most of the plants were escaped domestic species or weeds. Storms that broke into this prairie weather were prairie storms. They happened quickly and sometimes brought tornadoes.

One morning dawned clear as crystal, the white mayapple and dogwood blossoms like freshly bleached laundry in the woods, but by afternoon a storm appeared on the western horizon. Swifts and swallows recently arrived from the lowlands of Amazonia played on the winds that preceded it. In the ten minutes required to walk from the north slope of the ridge to the south slope, the sky took on the colors of a bruise—deep blue black, with sulfur yellow streaks to the east.

Swallowtail butterflies fluttered across the hay meadow, fighting the rising storm wind, seeking the shelter of the woods—emblems of fragility against the dark trees and darker sky. One by one they reached the woods and disappeared, folding their wings to cling to branches or trunks. The woods offered less of a haven for sturdier creatures. The big beeches tossed about violently, and the slopes resounded with crashes as rotten branches fell. The silvery beech trunks stood out strangely against the dark sky, and the underbrush of poison ivy and black cherry seedlings stirred sluggishly in the wind. The beech woods seemed empty of animal life, but this was an illusion. The raccoon crouched in her hollow beech with her litter of kits, and there were at least two fox squirrel families in the woods as well. If their trees broke or fell, they would go down with them—it is not unusual to find dead animals in storm-downed hollow trees.

All at once lightning broke the sky into three jagged pieces; thunder rolled and sheets of rain began to fall. In minutes the hay meadow vegetation was soaking wet, even flattened in places with the weight of water. There was no sign of the red-winged blackbirds that were nesting in the grass, but they had probably taken a beating.

The storm struck less violently farther north on the ridge. Weak sunlight seeped through the clouds and the rain fell more gently there. The old box turtle found the lukewarm rain refreshing after a time of dry weather. He idled in a poison ivy thicket, meditatively eating an oak catkin as though it were a strand of spaghetti. When thunder pealed, he pulled a little into his shell, perhaps an inadequate response to this atmospheric violence, but probably as adequate as any other creature's. The underside, or plastron, of a box turtle shell is hinged so that it shuts as tight as a box when head and legs are pulled in, an adaptation that may explain why these plodding, inoffensive creatures remain fairly common.

The short-tailed shrew and her litter reacted to the storm less calmly. They trembled as thunder shock waves rolled through their nest, insulated though they were by the overlying soil, and their tiny hearts raced in alarm. (A shrew's normal heart rate is numbered in the thousands of beats per minute.) The ears of the infant shrews had recently opened, so they were fully aware of the thunder. They sought security at their mother's teats, but she found this annoying since she had just fed them and was herself upset by the thunder. While trying to escape them, she injured one of the infants. It squealed in pain and crawled off to one side, but she paid no attention and left the nest. She was hungry.

She followed a tunnel upward until she began to encounter pools of rain water and hear the turbulence of wind on underbrush and leaf litter. She hesitated and took a fork that led downhill away from the disturbance. Soon it was quiet in the tunnel except for diminishing peals of thunder. The shrew heard a movement and hurried to pounce on an earwig that had also been following the tunnel away from the storm's disturbance. As she sank her teeth into its chitinous abdomen, the reddish insect curled around and tried to grab her with the pincerlike cerci on its tail. She slashed through to its ganglia, crippling it, and promptly began to feed, making hasty, crunching sounds in the darkness.

She returned to the nest with a full stomach an hour and a half later. Two of the infants hurried to her teats; the other lay on its back in a corner, dead from shock and internal bleeding. After the two healthy infants had been fed, she licked them over carefully, cleaning their fur to a warm fluffiness. Mother and infants slept contentedly for twenty minutes, then she awoke, hungry again. She approached the still form of the dead infant and began to lick it, but it did not respond so she ate it.

Above ground the storm had passed and the May evening took its leisurely course. The air was filled with the flower shop sweetness of dame's rocket—a lavender or white English garden flower that grew wild on the ridgetop. The woods rang with birdsong, although the calls sounded less clearly through the leaves than they had from the bare branches a few weeks before. Wood thrushes dominated the singing now, their plaintive flutings well suited to deep shade.

There were spots of extraordinary brilliance in this green matrix, however. Summer birds had arrived from the tropics, and the reddening rays of the declining sun touched a concentration of them in the lush woods of the north slope. Three scarlet tanagers foraged for green looper caterpillars in a black walnut tree while a black and white warbler ran up the trunk woodpecker-fashion, and several yellow-rumped warblers hawked gnats among its leaves. The fiery orange throat feathers of a Blackburnian warbler gleamed against the translucent green of sugar maple leaves, and the black and orange of a redstart in a pawpaw tree were almost as bright.

A ruby-throated hummingbird buzzed abruptly to the scarlet tanagers and seesawed in midair in front of the red birds, appar-

ently
scolding them
for not being flowers.
Then it bulleted away past an eastern
kingbird, a black and white, crested bird that
was hawking honeybees from around some buckeye flowers with audible snaps of its beak.

Beneath the leaf canopy the birds were less colorful but
no less active. Two Carolina wrens in a dogwood tree
scolded a passing opossum, intermittently breaking into
their rolling "Teakettle! teakettle! teakettle!" in their excitement. They had built a nest in the roots of a fallen black cherry
tree above the quarry pit and were afraid the opossum would
find it. Their noise attracted other birds. A pair of blue gray
gnatcatchers (which resemble miniature mockingbirds) cocked
their tails and made fussing sounds; a quiet, nimble Carolina
chickadee craned its head for a better look; a tufted titmouse
flew over, but soon rushed away as though too busy for such
entertainments. From deeper in the woods came the "cher-tea
cher-tea *cher-tea*" of the ovenbird, a surprisingly loud song for
the brown, ground-nesting warbler that made it.

An entirely different group of summer birds was active in the ridge's thickets and old fields. Electric blue indigo buntings and goldfinches in clear yellow summer plumage flew across brown expanses of broomsedge and goldenrod stems. The dry, exhausted old fields would not turn green with new growth for several weeks. On scattered saplings tiny, yellow-breasted prairie warblers threw back their heads, raised their tails, and sang buzzy, ascending trills in near convulsions of ecstasy. Their throats quivered visibly with the force of their singing: had they been mechanical birds, one would have expected to see springs and sprocket wheels fly out of them at any minute.

Other singers seemed slightly pedestrian by comparison with the prairie warblers, but they made a lot of noise anyway. Black-masked yellowthroats skulked in moist thickets, calling "wichity, wichity, wichity"; blue-winged warblers cried "bee-buzz!" from treetops beside the pastures; yellow-breasted chats, catbirds, and white-eyed vireos made an extraordinary cacaphony of grunts, cackles, mews, squawks, and lewd whistles from the thickest clumps of vines and saplings.

The songbirds were so colorful and musical that they seemed a little apart from Chestnut Ridge. They moved against a freshly minted background of leaves and flowers, and the darkness of soil and sandstone seemed to sink into insignificance beneath their airy realm, even though rock and humus were the source of the fruits and insects that sustained them. The songbirds seemed modern—bright, active, mobile—and, in fact, all except the hummingbird belonged to the most advanced of avian evolutionary orders—the passeriformes or perching birds. This is the order deemed to have diverged the most from its reptilian antecedents. Not all new arrivals from the south were so progressive, however. One such primitive was singing his "guttural and toneless" song (as described in one of the major bird field guides) from an apple tree. It sounded rather like someone shaking a ball bearing in a wooden box. "Ka ka ka ka ka ka ka ka kow kowp-kowp! Kowp! Kowp!"

The singer was a yellow-billed cuckoo, a low slung, brown-backed, white-bellied bird who kept to himself in the brush and treetops. Glimpsed in flight, he was rather handsome, with a long black and white tail, a gracefully curved bill, and bright rufous wing feathers; but there was something slithery and saurian about his demeanor that did not quite evoke the bright thoughts often associated with birds. A member of the ancient order of cuculiformes, he instead brought to mind the theory that birds are direct living descendants of dinosaurs.

The cuckoo found Chestnut Ridge a fine place after his lengthy nocturnal passage from wintering grounds in Ecuador. There were acres of thick, dank sapling brush to skulk in and thousands of fat caterpillars to eat. Yellow-billed cuckoos have evolved an enviable ability to ingest the hairy, spiny, often poisonous larvae of moths and butterflies, larvae which many other birds avoid. The Chestnut Ridge cuckoo menu included arsenic green cecropia larvae covered with red, yellow, and blue protuberances that made them look like plastic toys; six-inch-long royal leopard moth larvae resembling bloody bottlebrushes; red, white, and blue-tufted tussock moth larvae that might serve as Fourth of July fishing lures; orange, white, and black milkweed tiger moth larvae like Halloween party favors; pipe-vine swallowtail butterfly larvae covered with stinking hornlike bumps; and red-spotted purple butterfly larvae that resembled nothing as much as large, greenish bird droppings.

The cuckoo ate all these with apparent enjoyment, merely rolling them about in his beak for a few moments before swallowing them. When his stomach lining became too riddled or felted over with noxious spines and hairs, he simply grew a new lining and vomited up the old. The saplings of the ridge had reason to welcome his arrival since an uncontrolled infestation of caterpillars could strip them of their leaves in a few weeks.

After announcing his presence in the apple tree, the cuckoo saw a mourning cloak butterfly larva on an elm leaf and sidled along a branch toward it. The caterpillar was dark blue and orange, its back sprouting branched spines that resembled fire blackened trees, but it looked appetizing to the cuckoo. He bent to pick it up, rubbed it into shapelessness in his beak, and gulped it down. He blinked his large, liquid black eyes with pleasure and lazily raised his handsome tail.

The cuckoo glanced furtively at the branches over his head. The sky was becoming overcast as evening advanced: the storm had heralded a low-pressure system. It began to rain gently. The cuckoo reached back and rubbed his beak against an oil gland on his rump, then began preening his breast and wing feathers. A wood thrush that had been scratching in the leaf litter began squawking raucously and flew into a dogwood tree, where it landed with a boisterous flapping that knocked several flower clusters down.

The yellow-billed cuckoo took wing at this disturbance and flew gracefully and nimbly away through the tangled orchards on the ridgetop. He was in search of a female cuckoo, but none had arrived yet. In the last light the wood thrush delivered a few notes that sounded like "I owe Leo threeee!" and then was still. The dripping of water from the leaves became the only sound in the woods.

SPRING RAIN

The next day dawned cool and wet, damping the birds' ardor somewhat, although crows could still be heard mobbing an owl or hawk on the west slope. They remained enthusiastic in this pursuit although (or perhaps because) they had already built their own nests. Wood thrushes and robins sang on, oblivious to the rain, even stimulated by it. The robins made their characteristic rain calls, which perhaps express pleasure at the ease with which earthworms can be captured in wet weather. The yellow-billed cuckoo was also a frequent caller during damp times— cuckoos are also called "rain crows."

The cool rain continued for days but did not interrupt the ridge's myriad reproductive activities. They were too far advanced for hesitation now, and if by some freak chance winter had returned, there would have been mass destruction of the next generation.

New wildflowers emerged, less showy but more numerous than the spring blossoms. The ridgetop mound was festooned with large-leaved waterleaf and false Solomon's seal, each with sprays of white blossoms. In sunny glades hairy sweet cicely developed lacy, anise-scented flower umbels that identify it as a relative of the carrot, and spring avens—a rose family member —bore small yellow flowers with five petals. Bedstraw twined everywhere, its prickly stems and white florets tangled with profuse sprays of scorpionweed, a wildflower bearing masses of fringed blue blossoms. Flowering clumps of wild grape, poison ivy, blackberry, and multiflora rose completely blocked the old motorcycle trail along the ridgetop.

Songbirds built nests, sat on eggs, or fed nestlings in hundreds of inconspicuous places, while bluejays—themselves quiet now that they had nests of their own to safeguard—prowled after an easy meal of nestlings. The insect population explosions on which the songbirds depended were well underway. Invertebrate activities were somewhat inconspicuous to human eyes, since many individuals were still in diminutive young stages of their life cycles, but the sharp-eyed birds took good advantage of them.

The tiny nymphs of hundreds of bug, cricket, and grasshopper species were hatching from concealed eggs. Countless tiny spiders emerged from egg masses in which they had spent the winter, and equal numbers of harvestmen hatched from buried eggs. Mummylike pupae of the even more numerous flies and beetles twitched in soil, leaf litter, or quiet water, ready to emerge as breeding adults.

The short-tailed shrew found increasingly good hunting and began bringing food back to her nest. Almost full-grown, her infants had opened their eyes and cut their teeth, which made nursing painful. At first, the young shrews were frightened by the earthworms and insects she presented them, but they soon found it amusing to play with the semiparalyzed creatures during the dull periods of her absence. As the absences grew longer and the supply of milk dwindled, they found they could fill their stomachs with their toys and quickly grew stronger on the nutritious fare. They began following their mother out of the nest, at first running back in panic at the strangeness, but soon growing bolder. Less than a month after their birth, they were accompanying her on hunting forays.

The forest floor was hospitable to shrews during overcast weather. The mother and her two infants pattered across it in an intricate choreography of hunting and play, their movements so instinctual and spontaneous that there was little distinction between the two activities. The young shrews chased and pounced on one another as they chased and pounced on spiders and insects. Their dancing progress was a lively, pretty sight, although an ephemeral one since the shrews moved so quickly through the underbrush that their approach and appearance would be over in a minute or so.

The red-tailed hawk that nested on the east slope caught sight of a movement in the underbrush as she soared over the ridgetop one day. She flew stealthily to an overhanging branch and watched the shrews' progress for a moment, then dropped down and grabbed one of the young ones. She took it back to her nestlings, and the other shrews were not even aware of what had happened. They had been engrossed in devouring a slug under a burdock leaf. A few days later the remaining young shrew became separated from the mother during a nocturnal foray. It was unable to relocate the nest or find other shelter, and a great horned owl caught it before daybreak.

The shrews were not the only young animals facing danger at this time. The woods were suddenly overrun with chipmunks—the playful, foolish offspring of the February orgy. Evicted by irate parents, they ran about dizzyingly until predators had thinned their ranks and the survivors had established burrows of their own.

The old box turtle came ambling along the ridgetop path one gray day and encountered a newly weaned groundhog not much larger than himself. Juvenile groundhogs tend to be pugnacious, and this silky-furred little creature was no exception. It stood squarely in the turtle's path and made threatening lunges at the aged reptile. The turtle hissed and pulled into his shell, which surprised the groundhog. It became frightened—its pugnacity was an instinctual bluff—and began to tremble forlornly. The two were at an impasse since the young groundhog lacked the courage to run away, and they remained thus until the turtle regained his equanimity and wandered off in pursuit of snails.

In the old beech on the south slope, the litter of raccoon kits was increasingly restless and active. Their mother had to climb out and drape herself over a branch to get any sleep in the afternoon. It appeared not to be the most comfortable resting place for her—she kept getting up and trying new positions—but it was obviously preferable to the constant turmoil that issued from the nest hole.

As she slept, small raccoon faces would appear shakily at the edge of the hole, peer around as though in search of her, then disappear abruptly as their siblings pulled them backward. Spindly legs and fat, milk-fed bellies were upended to the accompaniment of squeaky growls as the kits tumbled over one another. There might be a spell of quiet, but then the clumsy explorations would begin again, the small incompetents squabbling and teetering at the brink of a fifty-foot drop to the forest floor.

GREEN FRUITS

The weather turned clear and windy, and the crows took to soaring high above the ridge and harassing the red-tailed hawks. The wind drove the woodland canopy into a constant play of light and shade—the maturing leaves had turned dark green and opaque, reflecting the sunlight as might a multitude of trembling mirrors. The branches bore miniature green versions of the fruits of summer: tiny acorns, hickory nuts, strings of bead-size black cherries.

On the ground there was a continual patter and rustle as the wind knocked down weak or insect-damaged fruits and twigs. Shriveled mayapple plants bowed under the weight of plum-size fruits, which would not ripen until late August. The fragrant dame's rocket flowers on the ridgetop were developing into curved pods resembling green shoelaces, and the white flowers of false Solomon's seal and bedstraw were turning into green globes of fruit. The fruits of bedstraw and of avens, crowfoot, cicely, and many other common herbs sported bristles or hooked spines by which they became attached to passing groundhogs or cottontails, thus assuring that none of the ridge would long be barren of plants.

Around the marsh thousands of green silver maple samaras spun to the knee-high undergrowth of jewelweed as winds shook the branches. The fruit trees in the abandoned orchards were full of tiny apples and pears, although not as many as in the previous year. The late frost had killed many of their just-fertilized flowers.

But the green fruits by no means spelled an end to plant growth and flowering. The hay meadow reached chest height and kept on growing, its yellow rocket flowers replaced by daisy fleabane, a sunflower family member with yellow disk flowers encircled by dozens of white ray flowers, and by yellow goatsbeard or salsify, which resembles a giant dandelion. The meadow's orchard grass and Kentucky bluegrass were also blooming. Their reddish pollen billowed in dusty clouds as the wind tossed the tall grasses. Scorpionweed continued to bloom profusely on the ridgetop, and three-foot-tall spikes of alumroot appeared almost overnight under the old apple trees. Clouds of bees and flower flies buzzed around thickets loaded with the inconspicuous flowers of wild grape, poison ivy, Virginia creeper, and bittersweet. In dry, sunny places masses of yellow cinquefoil decorated the ground with a motif once imitated in the borders of illuminated manuscripts.

Windy weather inhibited the noisiness of the songbirds somewhat—they found it difficult to sing with their perches constantly being shaken. Some of the birds had already raised a brood: speckle-breasted robin fledglings hopped about everywhere. Others were tardy in nesting, for a variety of reasons. A garrulous male house wren seemed to be delayed by an excess of enthusiasm. He zoomed about the ridgetop stuffing twigs into every nest hole he could find, including a mailbox made accessible by a shotgun blast. Sometimes female wrens followed him, eyeing his untidy offerings. In the normal course of events, a female would choose one of the holes, throw out the male's pile of twigs, and build a nest of her own, but this male was so energetic that he apparently bewildered or intimidated the females with his frenetic industry. None built a nest in his territory, but he continued his twig hauling with unflagging enthusiasm.

A pair of blue gray gnatcatchers had started to nest in a honey locust above the township road before the leaf canopy unfolded, but their branch had been blown down. Now they were beginning again in the same tree. They had put together a teacup of twigs and were hurrying back and forth with some reddish stuff they were using to line it. From time to time one of the wren-size birds would squat down in the teacup to shape it, prying at the edges with its beak as though scalloping a pie crust.

One bird species that the wind did not seem to inhibit was the brown-headed cowbird. Little gangs of these blackbirds continued to sing their rusty-drain songs and mate promiscuously in

the tree-
tops on the
windiest of
days. They seemed
more hurried and rest-
less in their mating than the
other birds, and there was good reason for
this: cowbirds don't build their own nests but lay their
eggs in the nests of other birds. It is believed that they evolved
this nest parasitism when they followed the herds of bison to feed
on the insects that the beasts attracted. They could not remain
in one place long enough to raise their own young and took to
leaving them with foster parents. The Chestnut Ridge cowbirds
were no longer faced with this situation—they merely followed
the Herefords from one end of the pasture to the other—but
their mating habits remained fixed.

The cool wind stopped blowing at the end of May, and the
scent of Japanese honeysuckle flooded out of the gullies and
brush of the west slope. Honeysuckle vines had completely overrun the saplings along the township road, and the vine-draped
trees had assumed grotesque shapes. On moonlit nights the
township road often seemed to run past a ruined city, a herd of
dinosaurs, and other mysterious shapes assumed by the honeysuckle tangles.

The song of the red-eyed vireo began to dominate the ridge in
the still, hot weather. For the next two months this inconspicuous, greenish bird of the forest canopy would repeat incessantly
from dawn to dusk a song that sounded like "See me? Here I am.

"Right here. See me? Here I am. Right here." The song would reflect the green monotony of summer as the prairie warbler's excited trill reflected the brilliance of spring. It wasn't summer yet, though, and the morning and evening clamor of birdsong was still impressive.

The sun rose and set bright red in the stagnant air, creating brilliant complementary color schemes of vermilion and green in the woods. This infusion of scarlet seemed to provoke the ridge's male cardinals. As the sun dropped below the smog layer and turned red, they would give their loudest, shrillest territorial calls, as though they saw other male cardinals in every red-reflecting leaf.

Another summer sound began in the old fields as the evening sunlight faded—the calm "treet treet treet" of field crickets. At this time, too, dozens of blackish beetles with orange-marked thoraxes began to fly above the fields. They didn't fly far, just a few feet upward, their elongated abdomens dangling below their legs. When they reached a certain height, they dived and their abdomens suddenly flashed luminescent yellow green for a few seconds as they neared the ground and began to reascend. They were fireflies. More and more of their lights blinked and bobbed above the fields as the sky darkened.

A jet roared overhead, visible only as an arrangement of red and green lights and a flare of fire as the engines raced. As the roar grew louder, a breeze passed over the fields and the jet sound mingled with the rustling of sassafras and hawthorn trees in the hedgerows. It seemed that the commotion might quell the fireflies, but they kept flashing, trying to evoke responding flashes from female fireflies in the grass. The roar and flare may even have stimulated them. Here and there, a flash from a goldenrod or teasel leaf indicated a female's presence.

SCRUBLAND FLOWERS

IN THE hot weather the dust lay increasingly deep and soft on the township road. Cottontail rabbits crept down to eat it —a source of calcium—and songbirds bathed in it to suppress the lice and fleas that were growing bothersome. Many other pests appeared as well as these parasitic insects. Black, yellow-backed snipe flies emerged in great numbers and copulated tail to tail on the dusty road. The fat-abdomened females dragged the lighter males after them, leaving wavery trails in the dust. The snipe flies crawled into fur or hair in an annoyingly persistent way, although they did not bite. The yellow-abdomened, pink- and green-eyed deerflies bit very painfully, on the other hand, and wise creatures shunned the shady, brushy places they haunted.

In the mature woodland, treehole mosquitoes and blackflies assumed the tormentor role of snipe and deerflies, adding the insult of their whining wing noises to the injury of their bites. In old fields and grassy spots hundreds of infinitesimal chigger mite larvae clustered in the shade of grass blades and goldenrod leaves, waiting to attach themselves to passing animals for the blood meal they needed to develop into adult mites. Both larval and adult wood ticks waited for victims in brushy places. They clung to leaves or stems with forelegs outstretched until they sensed a chemical exuded by warm-blooded animals, then let go their perches and dropped onto the passing creature. Chestnut Ridge sometimes seemed one great buzzing itch in this first spell of tropical weather.

The fleas, lice, ticks, chiggers, blackflies, and mosquitoes seemed to occupy a perverse and sinister niche on the ridge, a wrong evolutionary turning that it should somehow be possible to weed out, leaving a world untormented by bloodsuckers. Like weeds, however, the parasites were rooted deeply in the ridge, bound to it by myriad, inconspicuous threads, which could be connected to some unexpected things. For example, the male treehole mosquito, a nonbiting plant nectar feeder, is an important pollinator of spring wildflowers, thus the female mosquito's blood meals help to insure perpetuation of bloodroot and rue anemone as well as of mosquitoes.

Even if it were physically possible to uproot parasitism, the enterprise would be doomed by the difficulty of defining it. Scientists have been wandering in dazed circles around the concept of "an intimate association between organisms . . . in which a parasite obtains benefits from a host which it usually injures" ever since the concept was invented, and well they might. It would accord with this concept to classify the animals of the ridge as parasites of the plants since they usually injure the plants they eat. By this logic the pests and diseases of the animals are not parasites but antibodies secreted by the plants' soil matrix to hold the animal infection to an endemic rather than epidemic level. If the animals also benefit the plants by conditioning the soil, planting their seeds, or preying on other plant eaters, this is not untypical of well-established parasitism, which is always evolving toward accommodation since the parasite will not thrive in the long run if its host does not.

Indeed, if evolution has a goal or direction, the parasitic relationship may be the most important vehicle for such progress. Its tendency toward accommodation between host and parasite can result in extraordinarily successful cooperative relationships, even in the evolution of "super-organisms" from convergence of parasite and host. Lichens, with their unexcelled ability to colonize hostile environments, probably evolved from parasitism of free-living algae by fungi. Even closer to the roots of evolution, the chloroplasts, which make photosynthetic production of food possible for plant cells, may have begun as photosynthetic blue green algae captured and parasitized by the remote ancestors of green plants. The case for such a parasitic origin of the entire plant kingdom is furthered by the fact that chloroplasts reproduce independently of chromosomal cell division as might small organisms living in larger ones. Far from the biological outlaws they seemed, the bloodsuckers of Chestnut Ridge may have been the rudiments of a life form so profoundly new as to be unimaginable.

The yellow-billed cuckoo acquired a few bites in addition to his resident lice and mites, but he was not unduly troubled by parasites. He had found a mate through long and repeated song, and she was building a nest while he spent his time singing and flying about their territory in the ridge's abandoned orchards. The female cuckoo was very singleminded and efficient about her nest building, unlike the crows, who had seemed absentmindedly to drop half the twigs they brought back to their nest sites. The cuckoo flew ceaselessly back and forth between the hawthorn she had chosen as a nest tree and a nearby apple tree, carrying twigs she snapped from the moribund apple. The nest she was building so assiduously was very poorly made, however, hardly more than a flat heap of twigs lined with oak catkins, whereas the crows' nests were carefully woven and sturdy.

The cuckoo's nest was finished in four days. The pair copulated in their phlegmatic way, and the female cuckoo laid three greenish eggs at intervals of several days. Between the laying of the second and third eggs, another egg of similar size and color suddenly appeared in the nest. The yellow-billed cuckoo pair didn't seem upset by this strange egg, perhaps because birds can't count. The female simply began to incubate all four eggs, while the male brought her caterpillars and sat on the eggs occasionally when she went foraging.

A female of another cuckoo species had sneaked in and laid the strange egg—a black-billed cuckoo, the male of which sings "cou cou cou" instead of "ka ka kowp." Such nest parasitism is not normal for American cuckoos, but it happens occasionally. Yellow-billed cuckoos also lay their eggs in black-billed cuckoo nests, and since the species are quite similar in habits and appearance, little harm is done. The European cuckoo of cuckoo-clock fame always lays its eggs in other birds' nests and somehow has even evolved local populations that lay eggs the same color as those of the birds whose nests they parasitize.

The early June heat finally wilted the scorpionweed and rue anemones. Hay meadow plants topped out and began to go to seed; the yellow goatsbeard heads turned to white spheres, which blew apart and floated away as dozens of filmy parachutes. Heads of orchard grass and bluegrass hung heavy with seed. Most of the red-winged blackbirds that had nested in the meadow had fledged their young and departed. As the hay meadow lagged, the perennial herbs of the old fields had their growth spurt, the matted stalks of the previous year covered by a profusion of greenery—milkweed, goldenrod, dogbane, aster, teasel, ironweed, and thistle. Purple-flowered Canada thistles were already in bloom, and milkweed and dogbane buds were swelling.

Insect grazers appeared in thousands to take advantage of the scrubland growth spurt. Swarms of bright red aphids pimpled goldenrod stems, wagging their abdomens as they sucked the sweet plant juices. Metallic blue beetle larvae chewed on the goldenrod leaves. Gangs of burnt orange soldier beetles and emerald green leaf beetles crawled over the elongated flower tubes of Canada thistle. The thistles' leaves were under attack by pillbug-shaped tortoise beetle larvae, which protected themselves from predators by defecating purple masses of excrement onto their own backs. Black aphids and green, orange-headed leaf bugs had already eaten the large, tough leaves of burdock to tatters. The old box turtle made an interesting botanical find. Having become increasingly uncomfortable in the heat, he wandered north along the ridgetop until he came to the top of the deep quarry pit. He cocked an eye to look into it, and the thirty-foot drop did not look promising so he turned aside, his claws slipping precariously on the pebbly clifftop for a moment. He followed the edge a little way, then saw something attractive in the other direction.

The turtle turned away from the quarry pit and ambled toward a grassy glade that was screened all about by ash and maple saplings. At the center of the glade was a bare patch of earth with some tender green seedlings growing on it, and this was what had attracted him. Box turtles are known raiders of gardens. He walked across the newly dug clods and unhurriedly ate a dozen marijuana seedlings that some adventurous youths had planted a week or so before. Then he lost interest and wandered away, leaving a few seedlings to shrivel and die from lack of watering. Perhaps the colors of the ridge seemed a little brighter to him that day.

SCAVENGERS

The cattle raiser who leased the hay meadow came up to mow it. He was a redheaded young man with tattooed hands who lived with his wife, baby, and a half-dozen raccoon hounds in a decrepit brick farmhouse below the southeast slope of the ridge. After cutting a few swaths, his tractor ran into a groundhog hole and broke a front wheel assembly, almost turning over on him in the process. He cursed a blue streak, stomped about the meadow, observed the three other dirt-mounded groundhog burrows and hauled the wheel away to a machine shop. In the afternoon he came back with a rifle and shot one of the groundhogs.

A pair of vultures heard the shots and glided into a thicket of ash saplings beside the meadow. Timid creatures, they waited until the cattle raiser and his green pickup were long departed before venturing from the thicket and thus were superseded at the carcass by one of the ridge's red-tailed hawks. The hawk mantled the dead groundhog and screamed balefully at the vultures when they sought to join him, so they flapped away. Unable to lift the groundhog, the hawk filled its belly, then departed as the sun went down.

The partly eaten groundhog lay undisturbed through the long

June twilight, although a few bluebottle flies laid their eggs on it. A pinkish crescent moon began to glow in the southeast while an entire spectrum of colors hung over the cloudless but dusty western sky. At first the meadow's rich green was intensified by the reddened, darkening sky, but then it was obscured by the brighter green of firefly flashes. Most of these were made by the common, single-flash species, but there were other species that flashed in series of two or three, messages directed at females, which would be attracted by the characteristic flash patterns.

When it was quite dark, a female opossum detached herself from the beech woods and unerringly followed her powerful nose toward the dead groundhog. She wasted no time and began eating with gulping haste. Ten minutes later the large raccoon mother from the big beech tree emerged from the woods and approached the carcass.

The opossum turned toward this interloper and opened her mouth in a crocodile gape, the hackles rising on her back and shoulders. She looked formidable. The raccoon kept approaching as though no challenge was being given, but she veered aside suddenly when about two feet from the opossum's jaws and appeared to concern herself only with a few scraps that lay off to one side. The opossum ate even more vehemently than before, but somehow the raccoon kept getting closer and closer to the carcass. Finally, the opossum seemed unable to bear the tension. She turned quickly and waddled away, her belly scraping the ground. Besides the food she had just gobbled, she was carrying a pouchful of young.

The raccoon busily chewed meat and cracked bones for another ten minutes, but then she began to act nervous in her turn. She kept glancing up into the darkness of the beech woods as though she heard something approaching. Suddenly she turned and fled into the ash thicket but returned almost immediately to the carcass, whereupon a smaller raccoon came out of the woods and approached her. She spat and snarled like a cat, chased the small intruder back into the woods, then returned and finished the carcass, leaving only skin and large bones. After she had departed, the small raccoon returned and disconsolately sniffed the meager remains before trailing off after her. Perhaps it was her offspring from the previous year.

For all the greedy gobbling of carrion, it had been a strangely beautiful scene. The raccoons and opossum were silvery gray in the moonlight and moved about with a dreamlike fluidity—the grace of actions coordinated more by touch, sound, or smell than by sight. Animals that appear ungainly in daylight often have such a nocturnal grace. In particular, the opossum—a clumsy, ratlike beast under the sun—had a kind of hoary dignity in moonlight. She was like an ancient hieratic image of some dog-faced demigoddess.

Scavengers, which eat dead things, are generally considered less ignoble than parasites, which eat living, although eaters of death still evoke distaste, as though matters really should be arranged more tidily. Instead of leaving dead animals to be eaten by vultures and opossums, most farmers today bury them to prevent the spread of disease (one might ask if soil organisms and groundwater are more powerful germicides than the gastric juices of carrion feeders). But the ranking of scavengers above parasites in some biological hierarchy of worthiness is hindered by the difficulty of defining their roles, a definition that would require a clear distinction between life and death.

How dead is a carcass in which most of the cells still live and in which bacterial and fungal growth are flourishing? Would the carcass be more—or less—dead if the bacteria did not flourish, and it did not rot and stink? Is it a paradox that decay—by which we recognize death—is caused by abundant microscopic life, busily recycling the carcass back into other living things? The suspicion arises that life and death are not opposites as we tend to feel they are. After all, death is the driving force behind the evolution of life—if organisms did not die, they could not sexually reproduce for long without overpopulating themselves off the planet. For something to be dead there must be some life about it. We speak of the moon as dead only metaphorically, since it has never lived.

The ambiguity of life and death makes the ranking of scavengers as useful and parasites as harmful a highly relative matter. From Chestnut Ridge's viewpoint, the parasites that helped to keep animal and plant populations in balance were not less useful than scavengers that cleaned up dead matter. If the parasites were antibodies to the ridge "organism," the scavengers were digestive secretions, breaking the complex tangle of decaying life into precise molecular configurations, which could be assimilated by the complex tangle of growing life. In this sense the despised figures of vulture and opossum assumed a significance perhaps not far from that of vulture effigies unearthed from Woodland Culture burial mounds—effigies that seem to acknowledge that the eaters of death are guides along the way to life, and worthy of respect beyond what one gives to a garbage collector.

The next day the cattle raiser returned with a repaired tractor and mowed the rest of the hay meadow. Suddenly the mowed stubble was crawling with grasshoppers—small green ones with black-striped backs, large yellow ones with orange wings, pale gray ones that resembled sun-faded twigs. The mowing had concentrated an already large grasshopper population in the drastically reduced habitat of the stubble, and the local crows, blackbirds, grackles, and meadowlarks lost no time in benefiting from the development. Indeed, the alacrity with which they arrived to feed on the grasshoppers suggested that they had been expecting it.

The crows worked the meadow in a troop, two individuals perching in an isolated honey locust while the others were catching hoppers. The crows were obviously contented as they waddled across the warm meadow, just as they were clearly annoyed when the pair in the honey locust cried "C-a-a!" to warn them of the approach of the cattle raiser's green pickup. They disappeared into the treetops so rapidly that the young man was only vaguely aware of a few pesky crows flying off. The grackles and blackbirds ignored him as he loaded the last hay bales into his truck and drove away.

In a way it was unfortunate that the crows and the man had so little regard for one another. Their use of the hay meadow was nicely symbiotic, although neither party was much interested in the fact. The crows thrived on the abundant insects, which the cattle raiser fostered by fertilizing and mowing the meadow. The mowing maintained a high solar energy budget by excluding woody vegetation that would otherwise shade out the productive grasses. On the other hand, the cattle raiser would get less hay from the meadow if its wireworms, cutworms, and grasshoppers went unmolested. Of course, farmers can sometimes be convinced of the value of crows, but how does one convince a crow of the value of farmers?

ACID RAIN

A thunderstorm was approaching from the southwest as the cattle raiser departed, and the crows did not return to the hay meadow that day. A chipmunk on the ridgetop poked its head from its burrow and watched the storm clouds gather, then squeaked a warning and vanished underground.

At first the air was stagnant and the myriad shadowy niches created by leafy branches looked very deep and mysterious; then a wind arose and the shadows began to tremble and shift. Spidery reflections from leaf surfaces played in dark places. In the maple grove a breeze sweeping up the slope made the maple and pawpaw leaves stand and show their silvery undersides, as though thousands of green people were raising hands in salute to the approaching storm. Droves of maple samaras fluttered to the ground with each gust. Then the sun emerged for a moment and the sense of depth vanished abruptly. The grove became a bright mosaic of leaf surfaces, only to be flooded again by the next wave of cloud shadow.

The clouds were low and heavy, full of rain. They turned every horizon blue black, and when they burst, poured sheets of water on the ridge. They were also full of smog from the western cities, and an intricate series of chemical reactions in them had turned their water sour and corrosive with acid. The sheets of rain stung the eyes and burned the throat, although these effects were not felt immediately. It took several hours for the acid to burn its way into mucous membranes.

Captured by the ridge's screen of leafy vegetation, the polluted rain spread out and trickled gradually into the soil, its effects inconspicuous and incalculable. Probably the first to feel them were the redbelly dace, crayfish, green frogs, and aquatic insects of the small creeks. The gill-breathing fish, insects, and crustaceans had their usual difficulty getting oxygen in the silt-clogged flood water, but there was no way of knowing how the acidity of the runoff affected them, whether it was a discomfort or merely a strangeness. The fact that the aquatic animals were still fairly numerous in the creeks indicated that the lime-rich glacial till of the west slope acted as a neutralizer to the acid rains.

The dace and crayfish of the ridge pastures were at least healthier than their counterparts downstream, where the creeks had been channelized into cornfield ditches before they ran into the small river draining the area. It was unsettling to see the fish in these ditches. They were covered with red or black wartlike growths. Could these tumors be caused by the broth of chemical fertilizer, insecticide, and herbicide residues in which they swam? The eyes of crayfish taken from the ditches were often filmed over with whitish stuff, probably resulting from irritation by various pollutants in the water.

Given the conditions, it was a little surprising that aquatic life persisted in the ditches at all, and that there was even an abundance of it in places. A large school of warty minnows swam about a pool where a drainage tile provided a convenient hiding place, and a bigger fish—a grass pickerel—swam among them so rapidly as to be almost invisible. In clear, sandy spots tiny yellowish darters rested on the bottom, darting upward now and then to snatch floating bits of food. The power of life to persist in degraded habitats is impressive. But the fact remained that Chestnut Ridge was the headwaters of the small creeks and the downstream ditches. Gullied and silted though the creeks were by a century of soil erosion, they still had a comparatively unpolluted watershed in the ridge's woods and fields. Whether even diseased fish could have persisted in the ditches had the ridge been covered with houses and driveways was another question. The ridge's usefulness to wildlife did not stop at its surveyed boundaries. Who could say how far downstream the last drop of nontoxic water from its woods would reach?

After the rain stopped, there was no outward indication that something abnormally destructive had occurred. The sodden trees dripped for a long time and a smell of slaked earth rose from the dusty township road. Robins flew down to flop and splash in a puddle. A wood thrush and a pewee began to sing in the maple grove as the retreating thunder grumbled eastward.

The western sky broke into gaudy colors as the sun set. A slanting, navy blue smear of rain clogged the southwest and interrupted a band of orange bordering the deep purple horizon. Higher up, the sky modulated to powder blue, then to great swirls of cumulus clouds gilded by the sun—a pale violet disk in the haze. A moment later the orange brightened to magenta and the powder blue to aquamarine as the last direct rays of sunlight touched the clouds. The Herefords in the pasture glowed as this red light reflected from their hides. In another moment the light faded and the fireflies came out, more and more of them until they rivaled the distant city lights. A screech owl called from the ridgetop, the first since the end of autumn.

The short-tailed shrew heard the quavering whistle and paused a moment in her hunting. The hot weather had been making her miserable. Her nest had become so infested with fleas that she had abandoned it and wandered southward along the ridgetop. More wary than her offspring, she had survived two nights in unfamiliar territory, but the strain of homelessness was beginning to tell.

She burrowed rapidly through the leaf litter in pursuit of ground crickets that had begun their whispery stridulations in every square foot of the ridge. She leapt up through fallen leaves like a tiny porpoise and pounced on an unsuspecting cricket. The crunching sounds of her feeding ensued immediately, and a male short-tailed shrew with a runway nearby heard. He approached, and the female drew back and squeaked at him. He might have challenged her at another time, but he was well fed and comfortable in a large burrow system, so he disregarded her. The female crawled into one of his tunnels to rest after filling her stomach. She would remain in the vicinity.

There was very little rustling from earthworms—perhaps the acid rain inhibited them—but the better-armored insects and arachnids were active. Even more numerous than ground crickets were the full-grown harvestmen. They stalked about everywhere on their grotesquely long legs. Some already had parasitic red mites attached to their leg joints. The cliffs and crannies of the quarries were spun over with cobwebs in each of which sat a paunchy little spider sucking on a drab noctuid moth. An identical ochre egg case hung at the top of each web.

The woods were full of night fliers. A tattered luna moth quivered on a pawpaw branch, its green, swallowtailed wings

inlaid as by a jeweler with gold-
en, oval eyespots. It had mated
and its nonfeeding, adult life was
almost over. An orange and black tiger
moth fluttered past; and there were innum-
erable smaller moths—some iridescent pink,
blue, or green, some gray or brown, and some pat-
terned to resemble crumpled leaves or droppings. There
were delicate green lacewings with eyes that glittered golden in
a flashlight beam, long-bodied woodland cockroaches and fireflies—not as numerous as in the open fields but flashing even
more brightly in the shadows of the trees. From the township
road the woodland fireflies might have been lanterns moving
along the ridgetop, lights winking on and off as tree trunks concealed them. It was as though ghosts of departed cabin dwellers
were lighting their way homeward.

THE LONGEST DAYS

A spell of cool, rainy weather lasted through the summer solstice. The first of the yellow-billed cuckoo eggs hatched. The
nestling was a nearly naked, black, greasy-looking thing that
could barely hold up its head to beg for caterpillars. Being the
sole beneficiary of its parents' instinct to stuff food down a gaping
mouth, it soon gained strength and began to pull itself about the
nest with wing stubs and beak. Black feather quills grew through
its shiny hide, and it began to resemble a porcupine. Its move-

ments accidentally rolled the black-billed cuckoo's clandestine egg out of the nest, ending one small evolutionary experiment.

Despite the cool, overcast weather, the milkweed and butterfly weed in the old fields came into flower by the longest day of the year. The spherical pink clusters of milkweed flowers were immediately covered with colorful insects as though the animals had been developing in the buds right along with the flowers. The insects fed on the sticky sweet flowers or on the succulent leaves and stems. On a single milkweed plant there might be soldier beetles, milkweed tiger moth caterpillars, milkweed bugs, milkweed longhorn beetles, hairstreak butterflies, and numerous honeybees. Some of the bees became trapped on the flowers and fell victim to gold-bodied, emerald-jawed *Phidippus audax* jumping spiders. Most of the milkweeds seemed to have one of these hairy, nimble daytime spiders in residence.

One would have expected many more predators to be attracted to the swarming milkweeds, but the characteristically colored, black and orange milkweed bugs, beetles, and caterpillars had an effective defense. The colors were a warning that these insects—however fat and abundant—were full of the bitter, nauseating sap from which milkweed gets its name, and therefore not worth catching. The brilliant, swarming weeds were like Borgia courts, principalities thriving on poison.

The orange or yellow flower clusters of the related butterfly weed had fewer visitors, perhaps because they exuded much less sugary nectar than the milkweeds. Butterflies frequented them, and several plants had stout milkweed leaf beetles on their flower clusters. In damp spots some swamp milkweeds had also come into flower. With smaller, darker pink flowers than common milkweed, they hosted large numbers of leaf beetles and a few monarch butterfly larvae—white caterpillars marked also with black and orange.

Native plants adapted to colonize burned areas and other forest clearings, the milkweeds were accompanied in the ridge's old fields by a polyglot assemblage of other wildflowers. Teasel, oxeye daisy, Queen Anne's lace, and chicory were all from Europe, while black-eyed Susan, dogbane, and wild rose were native. In ridgetop glades yellow loosestrife and blue-eyed grass —both native—grew beside Deptford pinks and bouncing Bet—

both alien. The Indian mound above the maple grove was covered with native starry campion, while a nearby groundhog hole was festooned with its alien relative, bladder campion.

Of course, Old World plants such as chickory, teasel, and Queen Anne's lace are more commonly regarded as weeds than wildflowers. They had not been able to occupy Chestnut Ridge until the early nineteenth-century farmers had removed the forest cover. But they were not much different from the native sunflowers, asters, goldenrods, and milkweeds in overrunning the abandoned fields—both depended on disturbance of the forest canopy for existence. The only difference was that the alien plants were generally better adapted to the strenuous disturbances of agriculture. Whether alien or native, the old field plants had a hundred clever tricks for getting around the farmer. Mowed down, they sprouted from deep roots. Plowed up, they grew new roots. If their roots were cut to pieces, species such as Canada thistle (a Eurasian plant despite its common name) could sprout new plants from each scattered piece.

Although the weeds lived at the expense of both farm and forest, they were not really enemies of either, any more than parasites and scavengers are enemies of life. They were more like physicians than enemies. They took their fee—perhaps often an exorbitant one—but they often healed. They covered the bared ground and rebuilt its fertility. The prolific Old World weeds were like physicians with new, admittedly expensive, medical technology needed to control a new-to-the-New-World parasite—the farmer and his plow. Plants such as Queen Anne's lace have an exceptional power to reach into the subsoil with their roots and draw up nutrients otherwise unavailable to the topsoil.

A world without weeds would be almost as short-lived as a world without scavengers. Agricultural soil erosion would be magnified tremendously without weeds to hold crop borders with their roots. Soil erosion has in fact increased dramatically with modern "clean" farming, which makes lavish use of herbicides and fall plowing. Fortunately, many weeds are resistant to herbicides or are fast developing resistance. They may save us from wholesale soil depletion in spite of ourselves since we don't manufacture topsoil as quickly as we consume it. Chestnut

Ridge would have been a great deal more gullied, not to say a great deal uglier, without its flowering weeds.

Only in the mature woods were native wildflowers unaccompanied by aliens, but there were few flowers in the shade of full canopy. Virginia waterleaf, Virginia knotweed, and rough avens added scattered bits of white to the green matrix. There were a few blue spikes of tall bellflower and of skullcap. There were some ochre clumps of squawroot, a flower that does very well in woodland shade because it parasitizes the roots of oaks.

The rainy weather brought the old box turtle out of temporary estivation in the deep leaf litter at the bottom of a gully. He found hot, dry weather almost as inimical as cold and so spent much of the summer asleep in the moist ground. He climbed to the ridgetop and encountered a female box turtle. Experienced in the protocol of box turtle mating, he set off in pursuit of the orange-eyed beauty and aggressively began biting the edges of her carapace. She stopped and looked back at him, somewhat intimidated, but not enough to pull into her shell. He began pushing her, and when she did not object strenuously, he proved his mastery by clambering onto her shell.

The female turtle hissed softly and pulled a little into her carapace at this liberty. The old male crooked his neck and peered down into her re-tracted face.

They blinked solemnly at one another for several moments, then the male began nibbling gently at the leading edges of her shell. This seemed to reassure her, and she put her head and legs outside again, whereupon the male hooked his hind claws inside the rear of her bottom shell.

Throwing all reserve to the winds, the female pinioned the male's claws with her hind legs so that he was firmly hinged to her back end. Then he could begin the tricky business of rearing back to a near-vertical position from which their sexual organs could come into contact. Male box turtles sometimes tumble over onto their backs from this position and can actually die of dehydration and exposure if unable to right themselves in time.

The old box turtle was adept at this procedure, however. Applying his cloaca to his partner's in a leisurely but firm manner, he enjoyed twenty minutes of box turtle bliss. Then he disengaged unceremoniously and wandered off in search of food.

The female remained where the male had found her a little while, then moved southward along the ridgetop. She was ready to lay eggs fertilized by copulation with another male some days before—the old male was just an interlude—and she was seeking a sunny place to do so. She reached the hay meadow in late afternoon and found a suitably sandy spot near the assassinated groundhog's burrow. Conditions were right—it had stopped raining and the sky was clearing—so she braced her forelegs and began to dig a hole with her back claws. It took a couple of hours for her to dig down as far as her hind legs would reach, pushing the excavated soil into a heap behind her. The sky turned pink and faded to dusk meanwhile.

Five white-tailed bucks emerged from the beech woods and began to crop the meadow clover, which was already recovering from the first mowing. Differences in their velvet-covered racks indicated varying ages or conditions of health and nutrition. Two young ones had small, spriglike antlers; two muscular, mature bucks had spreading racks, one with eight points, one with twelve; and a spindle-shanked old individual had one large antler and one small one.

This fraternal order of bucks was a handsome sight in the twilit meadow. Their rich, red summer coats and white throats made an elegant contrast to the deep green meadow vegetation.

When it was almost dark, the largest buck lay down. The young ones immediately kicked up their heels and began chasing each other back and forth through the bobbing lanterns of the fireflies. Hundreds of the glowing beetles were rising from every part of the meadow. Then the cattle raiser's pickup drove along the bottom of the meadow, and the two young deer stopped playing. The little herd remained in the meadow, however, peacefully ruminating.

A splashing sounded in the darkness as the box turtle emptied her bladder into the hole she had dug. Then she began to lay her round, white eggs, which fell to the bottom of the hole with audible thumps. After laying each egg, she felt around with her hind feet as though to reassure herself that she had produced it.

She laid four eggs in two hours' time, rested awhile, and then began pulling the earth she had heaped up back into the hole. She was very slow and painstaking about this, trampling the soil flat for a long time after the hole was filled. When she went into the beech woods and crawled under the leaf litter to sleep, it was nearly midnight. The bare patch of sandy earth beside the groundhog burrow carried no visible evidence that turtle eggs were buried there, although an opossum or skunk might find them by sense of smell.

A screech owl called from the woods, its long wail dying into whinnying and rattling sounds. The night was warming and the stars were visible after many days of cloud cover. From bushes around the hay meadow came insect sounds that heralded high summer on the ridge—the long buzz of lanky, brown coneheaded grasshoppers (which sounded as though tiny men were crouched in the bushes making Bronx cheers) and the ringing trills and chirps of diaphanous, pale green tree crickets. A dozen miles farther into the Appalachian Plateau, where the woods were bigger and quieter, whippoorwills were making their tremulous calls, but none were nesting on Chestnut Ridge.

WETLAND FLOWERS

SUMMER seemed to diminish the movements of life on the ridge. Fewer birds sang, and not as many plants flowered. The monotony was superficial, though. Plants and animals were developing in so many directions it was impossible to keep track of them. The changes were too quick or too slow, too small or too large for human perception. Species kept emerging from inactive or inconspicuous phases of their life cycles to fill niches created by slight changes in the weather or by the emergence of other species. Others dropped out of sight or underwent such major changes of form or behavior that their continuous identity had to be accepted on faith. The ridge seemed to be mimicking the entire process of evolutionary diversification between its periods of winter impoverishment, populating itself with an ever-increasing density and variety of life as the warm season advanced. This mysterious fecundity made it easy to understand how medieval people believed that insects were spontaneously created from warm dunghills and mud puddles. Of course, the newly arriving animals and plants on the ridge came from eggs and seeds, not spontaneous generation; but the forces of creation were at work in them just the same. Each new generation was genetically somewhat different from all its predecessors, a brand new creation in that sense.

Most of the spring wildflowers had by this time vanished without a trace; even their seed heads had shriveled away. Fruiting structures that remained often had no apparent relation to the leafy plants that had preceded them. The broad green leaves of wild leek had disappeared, for example, to be replaced by stiff little umbels bearing fruits that resembled birdshot. At least the wildflowers left seeds, bulbs, or some perennial trace that could be located in the ground. The little chorus frogs that had been singing while the spring flowers bloomed had vanished completely. Not even biologists have been able to figure out just where chorus frogs spend their nonmating lives.

The yellow-billed cuckoo fledgling underwent an extraordinary metamorphosis after it had been crawling around the nest and bullying its newly hatched siblings for a week. At dawn it was the same black porcupine of feather-quills as before, recognizable as a bird chiefly from its beak and the wing stubs, which it fervently vibrated while sucking caterpillars from its parents' mouths. (It also made vaguely cuckoolike "cuck cuck c-r-r-r" noises as it begged for food.) But at midmorning the quills began to split open. The feather vanes furled inside the quills were unfolding, a process as imperceptible as the opening of a flower.

By sunset the nestling had lost all resemblance to its siblings. Its plumage was

completely unfolded, and it was a short-tailed facsimile of its parents. It sat and preened the new feathers as though it had always had them.

The brushy vegetation around the cuckoos' nest was at a peak of luxuriance. Blackberries had ripened, and the droppings of towhees, catbirds, raccoons, and opossums were purple. The old box turtle pushed his way into the brambles and craned his leathery neck to reach the sweet berries. Some of the middle-aged men who had filled sacks with morels in the spring now filled pails with blackberries, but there were fewer such invaders because poison ivy was in its prime. In some places poison ivy covered the ridgetop to a depth of several feet with a mass of trailing vines, green berries, and shiny compound leaves. One could (if immune to poison ivy) walk across such patches for yards at a time without ever touching the ground. In shady spots some of the leaflets were a foot long. Poison ivy carpeted the beech woods and formed a green wall along their sunny edges.

The greatest vegetative luxuriance at this time was in the marsh. It was so overgrown with plants as to be almost impenetrable. On its margins in the shade of the silver maples, jewelweed was waist high; it shot up over one's head in sunny places. Jewelweed is soft and succulent, but it clings and twines moistly around the feet. Clumps of blackberry and swamp rose mingled with seven-foot stalks of wingstem and ironweed and with thigh-high tussocks of rush. Past these obstacles, the creeping stems of rice cutgrass grew over saplings, fence posts, and isolated cattail stalks in a thigh-high mat that seemed less forbidding than the brambles and tussocks until one ventured into it and brown marsh water sloshed into the shoes. The spring water, fifty-five degrees Fahrenheit, seemed frigid in the summer air.

In the center of this green maze were the cattails, a half-acre of six-foot leaves and developing flower stalks, the sausagelike heads of pistillate flowers surmounted by narrow spikes of pale staminate flowers. The cattails grew so close together that the patch could be entered—with difficulty—only by turning sideways and pushing as one moves through a mob of people. This density seemed actually to inhibit animal activity. Aside from raccoon droppings, mangled crayfish, and a few blue dragonflies, there was little sign of it in the cattails.

Jewelweed blossoms were the main locus of animal activity around the marsh on hot July days. The lower petals of the pendant, orange flowers are enlarged into nectar sacs; these attracted a stream of honeybees, bumblebees, green halictid bees, and hummingbirds. The flowers' stamens and pistils are located on the top front end, and nectar feeders have to brush against these sexual organs to reach the sac. Hummingbirds got dashes of pollen on their foreheads while doing so, which seemed to annoy them. A honeybee crawled into one blossom from which the nectar sac had somehow been removed, the bee thrusting its head through the cavity as if in clownish surprise.

The luxuriance of the marsh was in striking contrast to the tree-shaded spring pool above it. A knee-high patch of jewelweed, monkeyflower, and horsetails grew on the wet slope between the spring and the pool, but a few swamp hemlocks and water plantains and a mat of filamentous green algae were the only visible plants in it. The pool seemed rather barren, but this was another superficial impression.

The pool was not a recently colonized, pioneer habitat as was the cattail marsh, which had been a cornfield a decade before. Its nutrients and photosynthetically fixed energies moved through more complex, longer established cycles than those of the marsh, where food chains tended to be short and direct, where cattails fixed solar energy and were devoured by crayfish or muskrats, which were then devoured by raccoons or mink.

In the spring pool there were two levels of food-producing green plants. At the first level silver maple and white ash leaves fell into the pool, decomposed, and formed a nourishing broth for diverse populations of bacteria, aquatic fungi, protozoans, mites, copepods, amphipods, and other tiny organisms. The nutrients released by their decay also fertilized the second level—growths of filamentous green algae and freshwater diatoms. Algae and animalcules served in their turn as food for larger animals—water beetles, backswimmers, water boatmen, water bugs, dragonfly nymphs, tadpoles, salamander larvae—and the myriad food chains were completed by an occasional raccoon, mink, or green heron. Trees, bacteria, aquatic invertebrates, algae, larger animals—there were so many organisms operating on the pool in so many ways that it was impossible for a single agressive organism such as the cattail to corner the nutrient and energy supplies.

The apparent poverty of the spring pool was really the thriftiness of long-established wealth. It cycled its sunlight and nutrients so efficiently that there was no surplus. In contrast, the marsh was choking in its newly acquired affluence of plant matter, piles of cattail and cutgrass cellulose, which its sparse and undiversified populations of decomposers couldn't completely break down. Silver maple seedlings were beginning to invade it, just as black cherries, white ashes, and slippery elms were invading the flowery old fields of the west slope.

As they moved into the pioneer habitats, the trees fostered ecological associates—root symbiont fungi and bacteria, leaf litter invertebrates, forest insects—which helped them to grow and spread, thus shading out the marsh and old field plants and inviting even more forest organisms. If the ridge remained undisturbed for a hundred years, the marsh would be a wooded swamp of maple and ash and the old fields would be covered with oaks and beeches. These changes seemed imperceptible and distant, but they were a strong current that ran through each day. Each silver maple samara that fell onto weed-choked moist ground helped to push the current along.

PREDATORS

As with the spring pool, the ridge's mature woodlands seemed barren in comparison with the marsh and old fields, but this illusion was dispelled directly upon entering them. One immediately came into intimate contact with large orb webs, which spiders of the genera *Verrucosa* and *Micrathena* had spun on almost every sapling and shrub. Having a spider web cover one's face every few feet is not a comfortable way to discover abundance, but it is a convincing one.

The spiders were extraordinary-looking creatures. Females of the commonest species, the spined micrathena, had garbanzo-size abdomens handsomely marked with black and white, from which numbers of wicked-looking spines protruded. An almost equally numerous *Verrucosa* species sported a knobby, orange or yellow abdomen with a silvery triangle on the back. The white micrathena, a scaled-down version of the spined micrathena, spun handkerchief-size webs in moist spots. In a few ridgetop glades the most striking of the spiders, the arrow-shaped micrathena, spun its platter-size web on weeds or shrubs. Its red and yellow abdomen ended in two sharp horns, like the vanes of an arrowhead. Appearing at the hottest time of the year, the micrathenas seemed invaders from a tropical jungle, and in fact most species of the genus live in South America.

The abundance of orb weavers indicated an even greater abundance of their flying insect prey. Black and green cicadas had emerged from brown nymphal skins and buzzed everywhere through the canopy. They sucked the sap of the trees, and the males made their rasping mating calls by vibrating tympanic membranes on their flanks.

"WWHHHhhiiiiiiiiirrrrrrrrrrrrr." It was the quintessential voice of summer. The cicadas seemed too heavy and bombastic to be caught in the lacy orb webs, but spider silk is extraordinarily strong, and occasional carcasses dangled from the webs.

Long-horned grasshoppers flew about on gauzy wings with slender legs dangling like Arthur Rackham fairies—the true katydids, which say "Katey did, Katey didn't, Kate did, didn't," and similar insects called bush katydids and angular-winged katydids, which make less distinguished stridulations. True katydid males would not begin to stridulate in earnest until August, but the lisping and clicking calls of their cousins were already joining the nighttime chorus of crickets.

Every kind of flying insect could be found in the micrathena webs—the webs were often full of holes from the struggles of trapped bugs, beetles, moths, or flies. For all their ferocious appearance (which has probably evolved to frighten birds, since the spiders are diurnal), the micrathenas were timid, sedate creatures that shunned turmoil. They usually waited until prey was thoroughly entangled to approach and wrap it even more securely in silk. Only then did they inject it with digestive juices and suck out its body fluids. If a human or other large animal blundered into her web, the spider promptly abandoned it, fleeing with her great abdomen trailing behind like the skirts of a Victorian dowager.

On the forest floor harvestmen were astonishingly abundant—

gray ones, larger reddish ones, even larger gray and white ones. The woods were full of small pattering sounds as they stalked about. Every leaf, bush, fallen log, rock, and tree stump had harvestmen on it. The spindly arachnids seemed to spend most of their time wandering at random, but there were flurries of more purposeful behavior. A reddish harvestman ran in tight circles around an oak leaf, pausing every few moments to drum its body up and down against the leaf surface. It made a sharp, tapping sound, perhaps some kind of mating signal. When another harvestman wandered over the oak leaf, the drummer quickly rushed at it and chased it away. The fugitive skittered across the leaf litter like a flung pebble, then paused in a hollow to chew on a mass of yellowish chitin that it carried in its jaws—the remains of an insect fallen from a spider web.

The humidity that fostered micrathena and harvestman populations was also favorable to the short-tailed shrew. She often left during daylight the tunnel system she was sharing with the tolerant male shrew. The leaf canopy was an effective screen against solar radiation, and even when a hot wind blew and tossed the treetops, the forest floor remained still except for the falling of insect-killed twigs.

Resting under a waterleaf stem one sticky afternoon, the shrew heard the whispery buzz of a bush cricket from a black cherry seedling and moved toward the noise. Harvestmen scurried out of her path but she ignored them. They were inferior prey: their wiry legs broke off promptly if grabbed, and their bead-size bodies offered little nourishment. The very abundance of the harvestmen helped to protect them, since with so many running about it was hard for a predator to focus on one individual long enough to catch it. Sometimes, however, large grackle flocks landed in the ridge woods, and the long-tailed blackbirds ran about eating everything that moved. The ground would be littered with severed harvestman legs after such an invasion.

The shrew arrived beneath the black cherry seedling, and the bush cricket stopped stridulating. His wings, which had formed a heart-shaped blur as he rubbed them together, folded back over his abdomen, and his antennae swiveled about in response to the smell of the shrew. He was a handsome insect with a mahogany-colored head and thorax, ochre legs, and a blue black abdomen, but not a sufficiently quick one. The shrew tensed and leaped the several inches to the leaf he was resting upon, knocking him to the ground and pouncing on him before he could hop away. The usual hasty crunching sounds ensued as she bit through his chitinous exterior skeleton to reach the soft muscles and organs inside.

Loud rustlings in the branches overhead made the startled shrew retreat underground with her prey. A vulture had landed for a rest in the quiet woods and was banging its long wings against the boughs as it sought a comfortable perch. It looked enormous as it flapped about, but when it settled down and folded its wings it seemed less impressive, hardly larger than a crow, and the expression on its naked face seemed harried and timid despite its powerful beak. Soon two other vultures arrived and settled near the first in the quiet companionability typical of these much maligned but basically inoffensive birds.

Toward sunset the vultures saw an old man and a decrepit hound walking along the township road. The old man passed this way on many evenings. He was a retired contractor who lived in a small ranch style house where the township road crossed the county road northwest of the ridge. One of the vultures became nervous at the man's approach and left its perch, rattling its wings against branches before clearing the trees. The old man looked up and saw the other two vultures, which flew away in their turn, heeding the familiar, mysterious warning of eye contact that makes the smallest bird flee promptly when a glance is turned upon it, and even makes it avoid the counterfeit eyes on the wings of butterflies.

The old man wondered what was dead, why the vultures had gathered. He sniffed the air and queried his dog, but the hound evidently smelled nothing unusual. The road through the ridge woods was a constant source of information and amusement to the old man. In the inactivity of retirement, it was one of his chief enthusiasms, and he missed little—civilized or wild—that happened along it, observing the traces of sexual rendezvous, drug dealing, deer movement, and bird nesting with equal interest. He probably knew Chestnut Ridge as well as anyone: he knew where the bee trees were, where the mushrooms were, when the nut crops were good. His knowledge went back well into the past, before the park agency had bought the ridge. He had trapped and hunted every sort of game there and probably would have continued despite the No Hunting signs if age had not stopped him.

He wondered if there was a dead body in the woods. It would not have surprised him. He had seen an increasing lawlessness in the township road traffic, and there had been several television news stories of corpses found in secluded spots of late. Nor would a dead body have disturbed him; he was familiar with violence, rather fascinated by it, as many people are. He carried a knife in his pocket while walking the township road. He was a sturdy, muscular man even in old age, with a ruddy face and a stiff silver brush of crewcut hair. His nose was hooked, and his eyes and mouth turned down at the edges, giving him a grim look. A pinched quality about his jaw hinted of childhood malnutrition, and in fact he had grown up in an Alabama sharecropper's cabin, only attaining Midwestern prosperity after the defense industry boom of World War II.

The old man had a bloodthirsty reputation with his neighbors because his conversation usually lapsed into monologues about his hunting on the ridge. There was a story about shooting four squirrels out of one tree, the point of which seemed to be that he had not wanted particularly to kill all the squirrels but had done so because "the old dog wanted it." There was a seemingly interminable story (which perhaps never ended because listeners fled after ten or fifteen minutes of it) about trapping a huge raccoon, which escaped by chewing off a leg, then trapping the same three-legged raccoon again; this time the raccoon dragged the trap into a groundhog hole from which the old man extricated it with a "twist" of grapevine—thrusting the vine down the hole, tangling the raccoon in it, and dragging the clawing, biting animal out to be clubbed senseless. The stories were told in a rambling, sometimes incoherent manner, with many gestures and sound effects, and the old man sometimes became so excited he foamed slightly at the mouth. It was no wonder the squeamish tended to fade into the bushes when they saw him coming.

It wasn't really cruelty behind his passion for slaughter, though. One of his stories shed some light on a motive. A pair of Canada geese had landed in a cornfield near his father's cabin one winter during his childhood. The family had never seen wild geese, and even after a great lapse of years the old man's telling conveyed vivid wonder at these large, edible birds dropping from the sky into the sharecropper's landscape of withered cornfields, unpainted cabins, and distant piny woods. Of course he immediately had taken a gun, stalked the geese, killed one, and tried to kill the other. The eating of the probably tough and gamy bird had been such a celebration that the neighbors had been invited.

The old man's passion for hunting was inextricably tied to food. If one stayed long enough, his stories did not end with the kill but proceeded to even longer, often fascinating accounts of dressing, cooking, and eating the quarry—how to keep opossum on the roof and feed it cornmeal until all the carrion passed from its system, how to singe off the hair and roast it with the skin on after boiling it with red pepper to kill the "wild" taste, how to serve it with sweet potatoes to soak up the grease. He seemed to know how to cook every sort of animal he thought worthy of eating. Hunger was probably the deepest source of his killing habit, and in this he was as innocent of cruelty as shrews and spiders, except that it was past hunger that drove him and present hunger that drove them.

The old man thought of going into the woods to seek what had interested the vultures, but it seemed unlikely there would be anything the dog couldn't smell, and the thought of spider webs and ticks discouraged him. He heard the rumble of an approaching vehicle and—taking knife in one hand and dog's collar in the other—stepped away from the road to avoid the wake of dust and flying rocks that followed a pickup going at least fifty miles an hour on the steeply rolling dirt road. It was not an unusual speed for the township road. The old man once had heard a resounding thump soon after a speeding car had passed him and had walked on to find the overturned car blocking the road as neatly as a tollbooth after flipping and flying some thirty feet through the air.

The dust cloud and the failing light persuaded the old man to turn toward home. He preferred to avoid the road at night because he didn't like to be caught in car headlight beams. It made him feel at once nefarious and helpless, as though the motorists behind their lights would see him either as a prowler or a victim for their own evil purposes. Often there were cars parked along the road at night, and sometimes as his footfalls approached such a car, the lights would go on, the engine would start, and it would roar away in flight from the mysterious, presumably murderous stalker of the dark.

DAMP HEAT

The temperature reached the nineties for several days as a low pressure bulge of hot air extended north from the Gulf of Mexico. The crows crouched in the hay meadow with their beaks hanging open and their wings spread, trying to circulate a little air through their gullets and louse-ridden plumage. Fledglings now accompanied them, and the order and decorum of crow flocking were sorely tried by the young birds' begging and squabbling.

Adults stood dourly next to blue-eyed youngsters (young crows do in fact have blue eyes, this is no metaphor) that gaped and quivered their wings as would newly hatched nestlings, making pitiful gargling sounds as though expiring from famishment. Fledgling crows will swallow anything dropped into their gaping maws—pebbles, sticks—and their begging instinct is so strong they will follow adults about piteously beseeching them for grasshoppers, which are crawling about their feet or even sitting on their heads. At times the harried adults would fly away into the woods, but escape was impossible since the young crows were quite adept at flying, if not at feeding themselves.

Chestnut Ridge was never as suffocatingly hot as the nearby towns and farmlands. The woodland canopy screened the ground and cooled quickly after dark. It did not store heat as did the rooftops, roads, and open fields. The humidity on the ridge was overwhelming, however, and the moist air that oozed out of the woods was a subtle erosive and disintegrative force as powerful in its way as direct sunlight, wind, or rain. It was so loaded with fungus and bacteria spores, pollen grains, and other microscopic detritus that it turned a shoe green or a shower curtain black within a few days. It made the skin itch and tingle from its prickly though invisible dusting.

The moist hot weather seemed a perfect condition for the building of new soil on the ridge. Plants grew quickly in the long summer days, and soil organisms worked feverishly to break down plant material into humus, but there was a drawback. The fungi, bacteria, and other organisms devoured dead leaves and wood so voraciously that they tended to consume organic material as fast as plants produced it. They continued to consume leaves and wood at night, while the food-producing chloroplasts in green leaves idled in darkness.

Activity in the soil was so great during this tropical period that it tended toward exhaustion rather than accumulation. The ridge's economy was subtler than conventional ideas of summer wealth and winter impoverishment: it included the proviso that wealth could impoverish. Less humus was formed during the dog days than during cooler weather. If heat and humidity had prevailed through the year as in a tropical rainforest, the ridge soil would have been a mineral sand covered with a thin mantle of recently fallen leaves under rapid consumption by voracious microbe populations. The biotic wealth recycled so efficiently by the soil organisms would have been stored in an astonishingly diverse array of living plants and animals, not in a humus-rich soil. Farmers who removed this fauna and flora would have found themselves—after raising a few crops—in possession of unadorned Blackhand sandstone.

Another aspect of the high humidity was a soaking dew on old fields, meadow, and marsh on most mornings. It became impossible to walk across them without feet and legs becoming dripping wet. The dew made the mornings chilly and uncomfortable but very beautiful. The old fields and meadow were full of the horizontal webs of sheetweb weaver spiders, and the dew condensed copiously on their sticky threads. When the morning sunlight struck the webs, grass and webs seemed entirely misted over with strings of infinitesimal prisms.

The dew evaporated quickly in the sunlight, and the sheet webs became invisible again to the benefit of their occupants— shy spiders that waited underneath for insects to blunder into their snares. Places that seemed like bogs at dawn were like deserts by noon—dry expanses of spiky stems and wilting leaves full of the creaking stridulations of short-horned grasshoppers.

The Canada thistles turned brown in the heat. The downy seeds blew loose from their flower heads and drifted across the old fields, a first emblem of the summer's inevitable passing. Small, warty seed pods appeared on some milkweed plants, while others were still in flower.

There were still new appearances. Brown, eye-spotted wood nymph butterflies and orange fritillary butterflies became common. Goldfinches gathered thistledown and used it to line nests they had just begun to build. In the driest, poorest parts of the old fields, broomsedge began to sprout from its perennial roots. Most of the year this grass's existence was evidenced only by dead stems and leaves of a beautiful red gold color, which gave the fields a certain distinction in the drabbest times of late winter. Now the bright green leaves emerged from the ground, their midribs delicately tinged with Indian red. Considered a noxious weed, broomsedge is a native grass belonging to the same genus —*Andropogon*—as the stately big bluestem tallgrass that dominated the virgin prairie. It thrives on dry, impoverished soil, and has taken over millions of acres of farmed-out land as if in revenge for the plow's decimation of its noble cousin.

GOLDEN WEATHER

The hot spell ended in particularly violent thunderstorms as cool air from the northwest pushed great masses of heat over the ridge. The air from the Canadian great plains was relatively clean, so the rain was not acid this time. One storm stayed over the ridge for hours, with flashes of lightning so regular and frequent that the effect became stroboscopic. Trees seemed to jump about in the darkness.

The storm built up during the small hours of the morning, when the female raccoon from the beech woods and her newly weaned kits were eating blackberries on the ridgetop. Unperturbed by the approaching thunder and lightning, the little raccoons scurried around their mother as though pulled on wires. When a sudden strong gust of wind lifted the pawpaw leaves around the berry patch, however, the mother and all but one of the young raccoons hurried into the trees.

The remaining youngster picked berries even more feverishly for a few moments, then it too hurried into the shelter of the woods just before a drenching rain crashed down on the berry patch. The raccoons crouched together under a mat of honeysuckle and listened to the raindrops popping on the leaves overhead. The spent drops then streamed down in gray, gossamer threads that wetted the raccoon fur but did not make it soggy.

Each rain brought different kinds of fungus fruiting structures from the network of mycelium threads that entangled every inch of soil and organic matter on the ridge. Purple *Russula* mushrooms pushed through the leaf litter of the woods, their flattened tops reminiscent of vinyl bar stools. Dozens of pear-shaped puffballs clustered on decaying logs, shooting out clouds of yellow spores if disturbed. Tiny *Marasmius* mushrooms that would have made good umbrellas for tree crickets grew directly from the fallen leaves that their mycelia had infiltrated. Hoary scums of white mildew covered the less vigorous tree seedlings and declining wildflowers. Most of these

fruiting bodies were ephemeral: they emerged, produced spores, and fell apart into repulsive black blobs within days. Some lasted longer. Artist's fungus on moribund oaks and beeches produced tough, bracketlike structures that clung to the trunks of trees for years.

It seemed strange that the fungus mycelia—submicroscopic threads that looked about the same regardless of species—should produce such a wide diversity of fruiting bodies, as though all animal species were to share a vaguely quadrupedal form and be distinguishable mainly by the differing colors, shapes, and sizes of their genitals. The fungus mycelia made up for their lack of visual diversity by the wide diversity of ecological niches they occupied. They were parasites, saprophytes, symbiotes, even predators that caught roundworms in nooselike structures of mycelium thread. Most fungi were adapted to particular habitats and conditions, and many confined their parasitism or symbiosis to particular species of animals and plants.

The fungi are in fact a great deal more important than they seem. Not only are they major decomposers of dead wood and fallen leaves, the fungi are indispensable to many green plants. Many fungus species live on the roots of plants, drawing nourishment from the plants' living tissues. At the same time the host plant's roots draw water and nutrients from the fungus mycelia. At some point in evolution the absorptive function otherwise performed by the root hairs of green plants has been partly or wholly transferred to these root-feeding fungi, called mycorrhizoids. The host plants keep the fungi from damaging them— from being "parasites"—by producing chemical substances that control the fungal growth.

This interdependence of root and mycelium is not confined to rare or unimportant plants. It may have been more the rule than the exception on the ridge. Plant-fungus interdependence is by no means completely understood, but it is known that many common forest trees—beech, oak, pine—and many common forest mushrooms live in this interdependence. So the great beeches and oaks of Chestnut Ridge were not altogether what they seemed. They were not simply trees—root, branch, and leaf—but dual organisms, like gigantic lichens. In this they were not altogether unlike civilized human beings, who after all depend on fungi—yeasts—to process staple foods such as bread, wine, and cheese.

The heavy rains scrubbed the air and ended in days of utter

clarity and brightness, golden days that became more frequent as the earth rolled into August. One could see very far west into the lowlands, where full-grown cornfields almost blocked out distant woodlots and tall hay wagons stood in newly harvested fields. Grackle flocks chased crows across the expanses of tasseled corn tops, and the red-tailed hawk pair joined turkey vultures and chimney swifts in circling so high above the ridge that they were often lost to sight.

The slopes began to resound with thumps and crashes as the first ripe apples, walnuts, and hickory nuts plummeted through the foliage to the ground. Starry campion flowers reached their peak on the Indian mound, and pink pealike flowers began to appear on spindly plants of tick trefoil (named for its furry pods, which stick to cloth or fur like ticks).

In open places members of the sunflower family began to outnumber the milkweed flowers. Deep purple flower clusters of ironweed marked the only conspicuous flowering herbs in the pastures, the cattle having eaten everything remotely palatable. In the marsh eight-foot stalks of wingstem put forth odd flower heads, a few yellow ray flowers curving back from moplike green clusters of disk flowers. White snakeroot began to bloom profusely in moist glades, its lacy flower heads and lush foliage a deadly attraction to livestock. Poisoning with snakeroot-laced milk killed hundreds of rural people in the nineteenth century. In the old fields the first of the multifarious goldenrod and aster species blossomed—fragrant lance-leaved goldenrod and heath aster with its hundreds of tiny white flower heads.

INSECT SONGS

T HE GREEN fabric of the August ridge began to fray noticeably under the onslaught of its insect populations. Suddenly the ridge was not a hump of unbroken green above the lowland cornfields—its southwest slope had turned a reddish brown color. The black locust trees planted to control erosion on gullied slopes were under attack by a species of leaf beetle. The beetles were about a quarter-inch long with a black stripe down the back—they looked a little like unshelled sunflower seeds.

Almost every black locust leaflet on the ridge had one or two of these leaf beetles on it, eating the soft green tissues so that only brown veins remained. The beetles were the same reddish brown as the destroyed leaflets. For an insect to be the same color as its host plant *after* it had destroyed it seemed an interesting refinement of protective coloration. It was an elegant color, though, and it gave the ridge a distinguished air, as of certain classical landscapes by Watteau. In the soft, rose light of sunset the ridge seemed a more suitable background for silk-clad courtiers on a lawn than for white-faced cattle and cornfields.

Other insect assaults were not in such good taste. Tent caterpillars had established colonies in some of the locusts as well as in cherries and walnuts, which were their usual victims. The grayish silk tents with their masses of caterpillar droppings took up half the foliage of some cherry saplings. The blue black caterpillars inside twitched and undulated as they exuded threads of silk, and the sight of a tent's several dozen occupants all doing this at once was an unsettling one. Equally disagreeable was the sight of woolly aphis colonies on the south slope beeches. The tiny, gray aphides attached themselves to young branches and sucked the sap, twitching their abdomens back and forth as they exuded a white, waxy substance (excess sugar from the beech sap) from their anuses. The sugar dripped to the ground and coated dead leaves with a gray layer resembling centuries-old deposits of dust in some forgotten cellar. On a chestnut stump near one of the aphis colonies, a yellow-spotted rove beetle larva also twitched its tail as it ran excitedly around a pile of raccoon feces.

Every tree, shrub, and herb on the ridge showed signs of insect attack. Whole branches of redbud trees were dead and brown, perhaps killed by wood-mining beetle larvae. Oak trees were covered with galls, oddly shaped red growths caused by tiny flies and wasps laying their eggs in leaves or twigs. The soft leaves of ash and hickory were riddled with holes and brown spots, and some black walnuts were completely defoliated by army worms—the caterpillars of certain noctuid moths. The denuded midribs of compound leaves that bristled from black walnut branches made the forest canopy appear bizarre, exotic.

On a mildly windy day a seventy-year-old red oak beside the hay meadow toppled and broke in half. It was so eaten away by red oak borer beetle larvae that a few inches of healthy wood around the outside of its trunk had been all that sustained and supported it. The rest was rotten, full of beetle wings and woody tubes where the brown, shiny-headed grubs had eaten their way through the trunk, packing the tunnels behind them with digested cellulose as they burrowed. The ripening apples in the old orchards were coated with black-spot fungus and riddled with pink coddling moth larvae. Another parasite— probably a species of mite —had caused scarlet warts to sprout all over the leaves of small hawthorn trees that had grown up among the apples. On the ground, leaves of snakeroot or crowfoot, which had not been chewed up by larger insects, were usually marked with wavering yellow tracks of leaf miner caterpillars—moth larvae that are so tiny they can live inside the thinness of a leaf.

The young yellow-billed cuckoo found these conditions quite satisfactory. Its parents had fledged it and then left the ridge, so it had to find its own food now. It had little difficulty in doing so: caterpillars, beetles, tree crickets, and other cuckoo staples literally dripped from every branch. Particularly abundant at this time of year were the larvae of the pale tiger moth—white, hairy, black-headed caterpillars with a fanciful resemblance to the white-ruffed, black-capped Pierrot of French pantomime.

The fledgling found one of these Pierrot caterpillars dangling by a silken thread from a pawpaw leaf on a muggy afternoon and reached up to grab it. Suddenly a sound like a wave breaking on a beach came from the tree canopy overhead.

"Shoom!" The cuckoo pulled its head back in surprise and looked up. A flock of grackles had taken off from the treetops, and the concerted impact of their first wingbeats on the still air had made the sound. Smaller groups taking off after the main flock sounded as though a fitful breeze were shaking the branches. There was a moment of silence, then a pattering as of raindrops began further up the slope where the flock had realighted. The grackles were hopping from branch to branch, knocking dead twigs to the forest floor.

The cuckoo again reached toward the dangling caterpillar and plucked it from its thread. Flicking the larva up and down, it looked around nervously for a moment and abruptly swallowed it. Then it began to preen and pick rather uncomfortably at its breast and underwings; the young bird harbored a fair collection of parasites from the untidy nest it had recently left. The grooming session seemed to make it feel better, and it fluttered a few feet to another perch, made a few gurgling-drain sounds, and flew into the treetops.

The ridge looked very different from above the forest canopy than from below it. The cuckoo saw a billowing sea of leaves, which seemed about to flow down and inundate the lowland cornfields and houses. Birds and flying insects occasionally broke from the green billows as jumping fish break from the ocean, and once in a while a squirrel would leap porpoiselike along the treetops. At night raccoons and opossums prowled the canopy, and to the birds and butterflies they must have seemed monsters of the deep.

The cuckoo fledgling looked pale in the full sunlight: its plumage was lighter than its parents' and it wouldn't acquire their black and white tail markings until after its autumn molt. It opened its beak and spread its wings for relief from the heat and parasites, but then it saw one of the red-tailed hawks drifting toward it and ducked back under the canopy. The hawk soared along, so close to the treetops that its wingtips sometimes touched leaves, and suddenly found itself in the midst of the grackle flock. The grackles immediately began to make their harsh alarm calls and to fly at the hawk. The whole flock rose from the woods and took off in pursuit of the red-tail, which flapped its wings a few times as if in mild annoyance and dropped away down the eastern slope.

With the grackles gone, the only sounds in the woods for the rest of the afternoon were the whining of mosquitoes and the peevish calls of red-eyed vireos and wood pewees. A few ground crickets stridulated feebly, as though enervated by the heat. Even the cicadas stopped calling as the heat peaked in late afternoon, starting up again only after sunset. A rufous-sided towhee on the ridgetop sang "Drink you . . . Drink your te . . . uh . . . uh. Drink your t . . ." Skulking in a blackberry thicket, he seemed unable to summon the conviction to voice the normally accented "tea" syllable.

As the daylight faded, tree crickets and cone-headed grasshoppers began to sing with considerably more enthusiasm, although their noise was masked until after dark by the cicadas' whirring. By then the true katydids had begun stridulating. After a few ungainly Bronx cheer sounds as the katydids warmed up their wing muscles, a clamor comparable to the crackling of live wires on a broken utility line began to come from the woodland canopy.

True katydids look rather like folded green leaves and stay in the treetops, so they are quite difficult to locate. This may help to explain why they can make so much noise and still be as abundant as they are. Like the smaller, twiglike tree crickets, they produce their song by rubbing a rasplike structure on one wing against a filelike structure on the other, but their volume far exceeds a tree cricket's. If a katydid chooses to stridulate outside one's bedroom window, sleep becomes highly problematic, although the song has a somniferous, in fact almost hypnotic, effect from a distance.

EDDIES IN TIME

When in full cry, the katydids completely dominated the other insect calls on the ridge. The insect roar even began to overpower the surrounding din of dogs, automobiles, airplanes, and gunfire. This had a peculiar effect on the listener. The rhythmic, incessant, sometimes syncopated stridulations seemed to pull the senses back toward some vaguer, slower consciousness. The florid, bizarre shapes of honeysuckle tangles and insect-eaten trees seemed more normal to this consciousness than the linear patterns of streetlights or the blue glow of televisions from nearby houses.

It was as though the twilit ridge imposed a rural, nineteenth-century imagination on the listener. There was a sense of dark, shaggy eroticism gauzed over with sentimental prettiness—the soft pink light of the western sky hovering over coarse branches and lustful insects. The assortment of eccentrically shaped deciduous trees that made up the ridge's silhouette did not seem to have much relevance to the twentieth-century mind, which is more attuned to uniform conifer stands, so the mind fell back on a kind of Currier and Ives sensibility. It was an eerie feeling, as though long-dead farmers were listening with one's ears, looking through one's eyes.

Summer nights seemed full of echoes from the past—candlelit rooms isolated in forest darkness, whitewashed plaster walls, the clink of a well bucket. It was odd that people who had passed away from the ridge as completely as the cabin dwellers should have left such a marked ghostly presence, and such an uneasy one. In contrast, the Woodland Culture mounds were quiet at night: their echoes could be sensed during golden August days and evoked physical contentment—villages surrounded by colorful squash and sunflower gardens, naked people in warm sunshine. There was little contentment in the ghosts of katydid nights—there was repose, but it was linked with disquiet, perhaps with sadness so deep and familiar as to be unconscious.

Ghosts might seem incongruous to an account of a year in the life of Chestnut Ridge, but the ridge did not always conform to conventional notions of time. Certainly it progressed predictably enough through its seasons, and there were periods in spring and fall when it seemed in full harmony with a linear, historical conception of time. The first wildflowers were lyrical, a golden age; the last leaves tragical, a decline and fall. But there were also periods when time seemed to stop moving forward, as during the bare months of winter and the leafy ones of summer. By geological standards these static periods were mere quiet stretches in the 330-million-year current, but they could seem like sargasso seas from the narrow deck of human consciousness. Many summer afternoons in the ridge woods might have been loops of movie film endlessly repeating the buzzing of cicadas, whistling of pewees, and sluggish quivering of leaf shadows.

Winters were even more uneventful than summers, but there was a certain dramatic tension in the wait for spring. No matter how empty the snowy woods, one could imagine a hundred heroic struggles taking place to survive until warmth returned. Not that there weren't struggles to survive in summer, but they lacked the stark dignity of winter. There were so *many* summer struggles, in fact, that the ridge seemed more gladiatorial display than classical drama. It was an arena so full of gaudy, violent spectacles that one soon lost any notion of the dramatic unities; and the insects, arachnids, reptiles, and other bizarrely armored forms that swarmed into the arena seemed less suitable as trage-dians than did the warm-blooded birds and mammals of winter. No coherent theme linked the spectacles of summer as the striv-ing toward spring linked those of winter, so time tended to weigh even more heavily on the long hot days. At least it did so for humans in temperature-controlled houses; the birds and mam-mals who had to feed and warm themselves through the winter may have had different impressions.

Given time's tendency to stagnate on the ridge, it seemed not impossible that it also might flow backward, as water eddies against the main current of a stream when entering a quiet stretch. The ridge ghosts were like the small whirlpools that mark such eddies—fitfully swirling shapes on the still surface of summer. Or perhaps they were mere figments of historical fan-tasy. Whatever their nature, they assumed a certain reality on the katydid nights. If one listened long enough to the insect songs, it began to seem that these ghosts also wished to speak. Whispers and echoes of human voices dangled elusively in the web of expressionless insect sounds. The lost wails of screech owls began to sound downright cheerful at this point, although the katydids almost drowned them out as well. The little ear-tufted owls were scarcely audible unless close by.

There were several screech owls on the ridge—a mated pair and fledglings—and they wreaked considerable havoc on small mammals, birds, and insects. On this evening they had already killed a chipmunk, a mole, and a white-footed mouse and strangely had left the uneaten corpses spaced out along the ridgetop path every few hundred feet. A young opossum quickly appeared to take advantage of this oddity, gathering up the limp chipmunk carcass and disappearing into the bushes with it while the owls threateningly clicked their mandibles at him from the trees. They listened impassively as he ate the chip-munk—the grinding of bone clearly audible from his thicket retreat—and as he emerged again, located the mouse, and crunched it up as well. He ignored the mole, perhaps repelled by its musky smell. Although not troubled by its smell, the owls

113

also did not eat the mole. It was possible that they were satiated on crickets and katydids. After the apparently jaded screech owls had flown away, the short-tailed shrew ran across the path closely pursued by the male shrew whose runway system she was sharing. Both twittered excitedly as they crossed the bare path and disappeared into the weeds, then doubled back across the path and vanished under a stump from whence came receding squeaks as they ran down a tunnel. The female was coming into estrus again, and the male was more than tolerant of her.

The two shrews ran along the tunnel until they came to a widening that was full of snails. It was a cache maintained by the female: mollusks kept well in the cool air of the tunnel. From time to time she moved out empty shells and deposited new victims. Hungry from the chase, the female seized one of the snails and began to devour the soft meat.

The excited male pushed and nosed at her, and she let him mount and copulate with her after the edge was off her hunger. He set his teeth into the skin of her shoulders as they coupled, a practice that may seem sadistic but which apparently helps to promote the sluggish shrew ovulations. Afterwards, the male sat up and pushed his penis back into its sheath—shrew physiology is such that a second coupling is impossible unless this is done—and they copulated again. Then they sat and licked themselves for a little while. Then the male became interested in the snails.

Another male shrew suddenly appeared in the tunnel, attracted by the goings on, and the three dashed off in a triangular chase, which ended a few minutes later under a log. The shrews ate up all the resident woodlice, beetles, and camel crickets, and the males had a squeaking bout, which culminated in the strange male falling over backwards in his excitement. The female wandered off, and the stranger found her first and copulated with her before the resident male arrived and chased him away.

So it went for several nights, until the female's egg cells had been shaken loose from her ovaries and fertilization and implantation had taken place. Then the female began to build a nest under a large piece of granite on the farther reaches of the male's tunnel system. She was not interested in being chased anymore, so the male began wandering around in search of other females and fell victim to a hungry screech owl a few days later.

The shrews' patterings surprised the grandson of the dead apple farmer when he stopped to visit the ridge during a business trip. He had lived all his life in Minnesota but had stayed with his grandfather at Chestnut Ridge during boyhood summers. It was he who had dug into the woodland mound in search of Indian artifacts. Now, walking along the ridgetop, he did not recall that there had been so many creatures scurrying about the brush. He heard the screech owls' wails and thought they were loons, with whose quavering cries he was familiar from Minnesota lakes. He had never heard a screech owl on the ridge during childhood visits, perhaps because those visits coincided with the heavy pesticide use of the late 1940s and early 1950s.

In a patch of poison ivy and ash saplings, he came upon the oak-staved water tank his grandfather had used in spraying his orchards. A spindly cottonwood that had grown on a damp spot rattled and rustled against the tank's metal hoops, lending it a forlorn, gothic aspect. A ramjet well below the east slope had supplied the tank, so there had been plenty of water for lavish spraying. He remembered his grandfather mixing DDT solutions in five-gallon cans, and the memory of its acrid, sweetish smell brought back his childhood summers as vividly as katydid songs or woodland smells. He had called it "drop dead twice" after the fashion among school children then. There had been a vague belief that insects could come back to life after merely one fatal dose of poison and that DDT had a lasting, special power that killed them a second time, as though what was later learned of the persistence and carcinogenicity of chlorinated hydrocarbons somehow had been intuited by young minds. Pesticides had been everywhere in those days—cans in the barn, dust on the shed floor, a whitish residue on apple leaves. The skull-and-crossbones poison sign had been a commonplace—usually ignored by him and his friends—of backyard fruit trees.

The grandson struggled through the brush as far south as the maple grove, where thumps and crashes advertised the retreat of one of the bucks that had frequented the hay meadow earlier in the summer. Deer had not inhabited the ridge during his childhood visits. They had been extirpated from the area in the 1850s and had returned only in the late 1950s. His memories were of a more populous, settled place, but of one already drifting toward wildness. Entering the maple grove, he found the fallen roof of a shed used for storing berries when the central part of the ridgetop had been an open field with a dirt road along it. He remembered the maple grove, though; it seemed not to have changed much.

Giving up on the tangled ridgetop, he made his way down through the cobwebbed emerald cellar of the maple grove and emerged on the township road, which he hardly remembered at all. Turning north, he walked past elm brush he had once seen in pasture and briar patches that had been alfalfa fields. The lights of the city sparkled in the west, much closer and more numerous than they had been thirty years before, although somewhat obscured by the brush. He was looking for a one-room, brick schoolhouse that his mother had attended during her childhood.

The schoolhouse was still there, just north of the ridge, but was so thoroughly surrounded by vines and saplings that the grandson walked right past it. It was getting dark anyway, and it was doubtful he'd have learned much about it in the shadows. It was empty and windowless, although the blackboards were still intact. After passing before the curious gaze of the retired contractor and his aged hound (who were sitting on their front-porch swing while the contractor's wife watched television inside), the grandson turned east on the county road and walked back to his parked car. He remembered a garage, a store, a bus stop, and an old hotel on the county road during his childhood visits. The road had been the major highway once, but another had been built, and the traffic that passed now did not even slow as it passed the remnants of the hamlet—a few white frame structures scattered among the suburban properties bordering park land. The fast traffic was intimidating, so the grandson did not linger.

RIPENING FRUITS

The hay meadow was tall with clover, and the cattle raiser mowed it again on a hot day in mid-August. The second hay crop was not as good as the first, but grasshopper populations were still abundant and there had been a great increase in crickets, including a species of ground cricket so tiny that its stridulations as it rubbed its matchhead-size wings together seemed completely soundless. Only during lulls in larger crickets' chirps and buzzes could the tiny species' whispering trill be heard.

Crows and grackles again took advantage of the mowing to feast on grasshoppers and crickets, as did a small skunk that had moved into one of the empty groundhog burrows. The skunk also pulled up large areas of sod to eat cutworms and beetle grubs on the plant roots. Luckily for the developing embryos in the box turtle eggs, she did not happen to sniff over the square foot of meadow where they were buried.

It was a good time for getting fat on the ridge. The black cherries were ripe—some were as large as grapes—and their bittersweet juiciness attracted many climbing and flying creatures. The raccoon and her kits stuffed themselves to bursting with the cherries. Honeysuckle, wild grape, Virginia creeper, viburnum, and sassafras also bore plump, blue black fruits; and dogwood berries turned ripe scarlet. The hawthorn tree in which the cuckoos had nested dropped large, coral red haws around its roots and seemed to wait for someone to come along and pick them up. The haws were worth picking up: they had a sweet, aromatic flavor, although the texture was a little mealy and each fruit contained at least two pink codling worms.

Groundhogs shouldered the responsibility of laying on winter fat with the utmost seriousness. A walk along the ridgetop always revealed at least one—sitting up on its hind legs to eat an apple corn-on-the-cob fashion or crouching to graze on sweet cicely. An old black-faced groundhog that lived above the quarry pit retreated promptly into its burrow if it saw an intruder, but a younger individual farther south merely paused a moment, sighed, and began to eat again, unwilling to abandon its pleasures. The ranginess of ear and shank of a cottontail grazing nearby was in sharp contrast to the roly-poly young groundhog, which already had so much fat mantling its shoulders that it was neckless and distinctly top-heavy. When it finally did take alarm and flee, the shoulder fat bounced back and forth in a suety counterpoint to the movements of bone and muscle.

Mayapples began to ripen after hanging on withered stems all summer. They tasted like pineapple lifesavers. A very few banana-shaped pawpaw fruits hung on the little trees—it wasn't a good year for pawpaws—but their orange, custardy flesh wouldn't ripen until September. False Solomon's seal fruits turned from pink to red, and the scarlet berries of a jack-in-the-pulpit were suddenly conspicuous. Prickly fruits of burdock and tick trefoil waited to be transported by some animal to a likely seedbed. The jewelweeds around the marsh were less passive. When a breeze or passerby jarred their fruits, the translucent green capsules exploded like overcharged cannons and shot the soft, bumpy seeds several feet. The seeds were a lovely pale blue color inside and tasted like walnuts. The jewelweeds continued to grow and flower even as the seeds ripened. They were annuals, completely dependent on their seeds for survival of the species into the next year.

True sunflowers blossomed in late August. Jerusalem artichokes with several flower heads and huge coarse leaves stood nine feet tall on a sunny mound near the hay meadow. Four-foot-tall woodland sunflowers poked through the reddening leaves of ridgetop poison ivy thickets. Green-headed coneflowers raised their golden-rayed flowers in moist gullies and glades. The coarse, aromatic sunflowers seemed peculiar emblems of green vegetation's approaching death on the ridge—the delicate, white bloodroot and rue anemones of spring would have suited better the traditional drooping-lily notion of mortality. But the radiant sun is no more alive than the pale moon, and the earth will as likely end in fire as ice, so a sunflower is as suitable an emblem of annihilation as any.

Many other sunflower family plants bloomed late, as though they'd been waiting for insects to prune the earlier vegetation. Plumelike Canada goldenrod and showy New England aster appeared in the old fields. Zigzag wands of blue-stemmed goldenrod flowered in the woods. Along the edges of the woods grew white wood asters, their large heart-shaped leaves adapted to capture all available light, in contrast to the small leaves of the field asters.

In a few grassy spots the ridge's only surviving orchid species came into flower—slender ladies' tresses. Its white flowers were the size of apple seeds, hardly candidates for the collector's hothouse. One had to get down on hands and knees and sort carefully through the grass to locate the foot-high spikes on which the flowers were spirally arranged.

One warm afternoon a yellow crab spider crouched on a ladies' tresses spike with its pincerlike forelegs open, waiting for tiny flies attracted by the blossoms to come within reach. A ladybird beetle larva resembling an orange and black concertina was climbing up the same orchid. When they met, it was the spider that fled—ladybird larvae are quite ferocious and will attack anything, from the aphids upon which they usually prey to a human being. Someone sitting in grass where the larvae are numerous will receive many painful little pinches. The crab spider lowered itself to the ground on a thread of silk and hurried off in search of another flower, passing a black treehopper with a large hornlike protuberance on its front end. Oblivious to the spider, the well-armored treehopper climbed a grass blade in its top-heavy, hobbyhorse way, then climbed down again.

A pinkish gray miasma covered the sky: a thunderstorm was

approaching, but it was a vague, fitful disturbance compared to the galloping storms of the spring. There was no thunder at all for a long time after the sky became dark, only a faint breeze and a peculiar, diffused light that turned smoky orange as the cloud-hidden sun sank lower. Then the breeze freshened and pulled in earnest at insect-tattered leaves of black walnut. Many of the leaflets began to fall. They leaped skyward as the wind snapped their petioles, rose spinning until the gust that lifted them played itself out, then drifted obliquely to the ground, settling into the leaf litter with whispering sounds.

The strange orange light intensified as thunder began. The rumbles and flashes were faint, seeming to come from high in the clouds, but it began to rain hard anyway. The light turned an extraordinary apricot yellow; the outlines of the trees were a sepia brown tiny against it. Then the sun set and the apricot modulated to a more normal pink. Gray clumps of cumulus appeared and spread until the western horizon was the color of slate. The thunder ceased, and crickets and an occasional katydid began to call, responding perhaps to the changes in air pressure.

A few fireflies still flashed their cold green lights in the woods, but much more numerous now were their larvae, which resembled stubby millipedes and crawled on the ground. Some had luminescent abdomens, although they did not flash as brightly as the adults. Instead they glowed with a light so soft that they were conspicuous only on cloudy nights. They seemed to be everywhere on this warm, moist evening—wandering green or yellow glows that often faded mysteriously as the observer approached and the frightened larva took refuge under a stone.

After midnight the sky suddenly cleared and the temperature dropped lower than it had since May. The firefly larvae disappeared into the ground, and there were no more lights in the woods. Katydid songs slowed and stopped, and the trills and lisps of tree crickets and false katydids became languid and feeble, then stopped in their turn. Screech owl calls and an ominously dry rattling of leaves in the wind were the only sounds on the ridge.

The next morning was chilly and quiet, but a bright sun had the ground crickets singing again by noon. Waves of fleecy cumulus clouds drifted over from the northwest, and the wind carried a variety of migrants. Flocks of nighthawks flapped along, tilting and rocking on long wings. Sometimes they paused in their generally southward movement (some flocks were flying north for some reason) and spiraled upward until they reached the limits of vision and resembled clouds of gnats circling at treetop level. Urbanized relatives of whippoorwills, the nighthawks had left nesting sites on shopping center roofs to begin their fall migration to the Amazon basin. Another long-winged bird flew high over the ridge, drifting southward in great looping circles that perhaps took advantage of some complex air pattern—an osprey. Other migrants moved closer to the earth. A Cooper's hawk caught a juvenile cardinal above the Indian mound, leaving a splash of gray and scarlet feathers on white snakeroot blossoms. A large flight of monarch butterflies paused for the night in the treetops before proceeding toward Mexican wintering grounds. The setting sun colored ash and oak leaves the same orange as the butterflies.

WARM MISTS

Early September was a luxurious time. The air was warm and moist but not hot and sticky, quiet but not stifling. The tangles of poison ivy and wild grape had thinned somewhat, and fewer biting insects were active. Early-turning leaves echoed the brilliance of late-blooming flowers, and the air was rich with pleasant smells—ripe apples, aromatic herbs, fallen leaves.

The ridge's scattered abundances usually came where one thing gradually merged into another. More wildlife was found on the edges of old fields, marsh, and woods than in the centers. Thickets of food plants between woodland shade and open fields attracted animals from both habitats, as well as creatures such as quail and rabbits that live almost entirely in such transition zones. The spaces between the shady woods and the bright fields were a little like the transition from the green effulgence of summer to the colorful ripening of fall—both offered the organism a temporary balance between the demands and promises of divergent environments.

To a great extent organisms depend on such times of balance for their continuation. If life was all a frenzy of change, it would wear itself out as tropical soils can exhaust themselves by the vigor of their decomposition. Vague stretches of quiescence are as important to survival as growth. At this time of year the ridge often had a dreamlike suspended air, as though food production and storing were carried on as afterthoughts while life underwent a psychic renewal such as dreams provide. This suspension did not seem airless and static as had the earlier stagnant periods of high summer. There was much change, but it was gentle, as with the gradual withering and yellowing of the underbrush, which made the woods seem open and airy, not barren.

The cicadas began to die: they fell to earth, buzzed and blundered a little while, then were quiet. Their metallic-colored bodies and bulging, glassy eyes made them resemble clockwork toys that someone had forgotten to wind up. Other insects were just coming to full strength. More honeybees and bumblebees than ever buzzed about the goldenrods and asters, their abdomens dusted with pollen. Black-and-yellow-banded locust borer beetles with extravagantly long antennae sat on the goldenrods and ate pollen. Fat milkweed pods were under attack by milkweed bug nymphs, ranging from aphid to firefly size; the fast-growing young bugs had sucked some of the pods withered and purple.

Late one afternoon underground ant colonies began sending

out their young queens. One after another the fertile females emerged from the antholes and flew upward on transparent wings that glittered in the soft sunlight. A large, purplish toad sat beside an ant hole, snapping up the young queens and males as they emerged for their nuptial flight. The stout, popeyed amphibian lacked only a toga and olive wreath to resemble a Roman gourmand feasting on songbirds. Obviously enjoying himself immensely, the toad did not budge from the spot until the last winged ant had emerged. There was an audible snap each time he closed his mouth on one. Sometimes he brushed his mouth with a foreleg to push down an imperfectly swallowed wing.

It was a good time for predators on insects, since the prey were full-grown and often unwary with satiety or sexual excitement. In the old fields yellow and black *Argiope* spiders with abdomens the size of quarters spun two-foot-diameter orb webs among the goldenrod stems. Silk-wrapped mummies of honeybees and grasshoppers littered the ground under the webs. Each goldenrod plume seemed to have a resident green-jawed *Phiddipus audax* jumping spider now that the milkweeds had gone to seed. *Micrathena* webs were still thick in the woods. The short-tailed shrew, who had given birth to a litter of six healthy infants, found hundreds of insects around odorous piles of rotting apples in the old orchards. Many were drunk with the fermenting juices and easy to catch, even baldfaced hornets with

their poisonous stings. The
shrew sometimes caught female
crickets or beetles in the act of
laying their eggs. With their ovipositors buried in the soil or plant
stems, they were easy prey, even a brown *Prionus* beetle almost
as large as the shrew. Producing milk for six infants was a great
drain on the shrew's energy, though, and she barely kept ahead
of her hunger no matter how much she ate.

Many other vertebrates became unusually active and visible
as they enjoyed the late summer abundance. Squirrels, jays, and
chipmunks rushed about gathering and hoarding beechnuts and
acorns. Fox squirrels went into meadows and pastures to bury
nuts, patting turf down over their treasures with a flurry of fore-
paws and a vacant expression, as though wondering why they
were going to so much trouble. Bluejays were less assiduous
about their hoarding, carrying the acorns about for unnecessary
lengths of time, sometimes dropping them absentmindedly. One
jay seemed to think it could safeguard an acorn very well by
pulling a leaf over it.

A second crop of young chipmunks was kicked out into the
world, and individual chipmunks became increasingly proprie-
tary about their living quarters. They crouched outside their inconspicuous burrow entrances making drowsy "tok, tok" sounds,
which were answered from neighboring burrows. Sometimes

there were duels of "toks," each individual trying to call louder and faster than its neighbor, but these didn't last long. The participants usually trailed off sleepily after a few minutes. Although they were perhaps unaware of why they fought these verbal duels, the effect was to lay claim to the burrow and food store each would need to get through the winter.

The old turtle's response to the shortening days was less structured than the mammals'. He was more active than in July, but only because the weather was less hot and dry. If a September night grew chilly, he simply crawled a little deeper into his bed of leaf litter and came out later in the morning. Under no obligation to store food or put on winter fat, he took the abundance of fruits and insects in stride, simply spending less time in search of food and more resting in the sunlight. The ridge's snakes also spent more time basking than they had in the summer, and it was not unusual to find black snakes and water snakes extended full length on sunny logs. They let themselves be approached closely, or even touched, before vibrating their tails in annoyance and whisking away into the weeds.

The retired contractor's wife encountered a snake while collecting apples in the abandoned orchards. It was a little yellow-striped garter snake, basking among knobby roots and tufts of moss beneath a decrepit McIntosh, oblivious to the drunken hornets that bumbled around it. It didn't move when the old woman approached, merely flicked out its red tongue a few times. Neither she nor her husband were snake-killers (unless they found one near their house), and the woman only scraped her foot across the ground near the snake when she saw it, partly to drive it away, partly in curiosity to see what it might do. It still didn't move. She touched it gently with her foot, and it leapt into action, crawling down a hole among the roots. It paused a moment with just its tail visible, then continued out of sight. The old woman watched in fascination. Snake holes are common features of country lore, but it is unusual to see a snake actually disappear into one (even more unusual to see a snake emerge).

The old woman had something in common with snakes: she was deaf. (Snakes lack external ears, but compensate by sensing ground vibrations with their entire bodies.) She led a solitary life, accordingly. Her deafness was that of old age, and she wasn't able to compensate for it by lip reading or sign language. When she talked with people, she spoke very loud, as though by raising her own voice she might amplify other sounds, but the only effect of this was that she could hear her own words. The replies of others remained mostly unintelligible to her. In compensation the visual world had assumed great importance. She still watched television at night from habit, but the frustration of trying to interpret its cryptic images had increased her interest in the actual world. She spent considerable time watching the ridge to see what events it might bring her. When she went to gather apples, she moved quietly and saw rabbits, squirrels, and sometimes deer nibbling the fallen fruit.

She was impressed with the beauty of these creatures: they seemed innocent to her, childlike. It had sometimes angered her when her husband had killed them so determinedly. The shooting of four squirrels from the same tree had been a source of bitterness between them; according to the old man's monologue, she had almost thrown him out of the house because of it. But rabbits sometimes got into her garden, and she didn't mind so much if her husband shot them then. She felt a not unusual ambivalence toward wild animals. She could regard a rabbit as a furry friend at one moment, as a mangy garden raider at the next, and not be too much troubled by the discrepancy.

Moving slowly, she filled her shopping bag with apples. She was stocky and sharp-featured like her husband, but seemed less healthy, perhaps from a lifetime of bearing children and working indoors. She had difficulty bending to pick through the apples, so many of which were ruined by bruises or insects. She looked back with nostalgia on the days when the orchard had been tended, sharing with many country people a disapproval of farmland reverting to wildness, even though this benefits the game and songbirds they value (and though she had not been able to collect free apples when the orchard had been in commercial production).

When the shopping bag was full, she rested awhile and looked around her. Glancing at a small sassafras tree, she saw a five-inch-long, red-dotted green caterpillar (a luna moth caterpillar) and felt a small shock of repulsion. It was chewing on a leaf with rapid, machinelike motions of its jaws while a clear, oily liquid dripped from its body. Her glance wandered to the next branch and encountered a copulating pair of walkingsticks—brown and green, wingless insects that look like six-legged sticks. The skinny male crouched on the much stouter female's back, gripping the end of her abdomen with forcepslike cerci on the end of his. The pair was motionless, rapt in an erotic trance. After finding five such pairs on the sassafras, the old woman stopped counting and decided she had had enough of the ridge for that day. She went home to make applesauce. Later in the fall, if her hearing had been better, she might have become aware of a faint pattering sound as thousands of walkingstick eggs dropped from females' abdomens and fell to the forest floor.

The first autumn rain came one night in mid-September after dark clouds had built up through the afternoon. It began falling so softly that it seemed almost illusory, but welcome and somehow comforting, like the first lull of forgetfulness one feels while drifting into sleep. It was a warm rain and the tree crickets sang through it, although the katydids seemed depressed by it and called infrequently. The great horned owls began to call again after months of silence. One rather high-pitched voice, probably the female's, called "Hoo hoo *hoo* hoo hoo" and a very deep, saturnine voice answered "Hoo *hoo* hoo hoo. Hoo hoo hoo." A screech owl whinnied nearby, as though unwilling to relinquish its summer possession of the ridge.

For several days the ridge floated in a void as gray and indistinct as the backgrounds of Chinese paintings. Goldenrod and aster stems leaned at odd angles under a heavy weight of raindrops and the *Argiope* webs between them were elaborate networks of glass beads. Every flower and leaf was precisely delineated against the misty background. Red dogwood berries flared into electric brilliance at ten feet of distance and faded into insignificance at twenty. The western lowland was hidden by a mist screen that turned red and blue during the sunset but was otherwise quite featureless. Animals and their calls popped in and out of the gray background with a peculiar emphasis. One moment a slope would be quite still except for the dripping of water from the trees, then the zany rattle of a flicker would echo through the woods as through an empty theater.

One misty afternoon a strange call resounded in the south

slope beech woods —a scream ending in a squawk. A sharp-shinned hawk dropped off a branch and shot through the foliage in pursuit of a bluejay, which it chased in a zigzag course until both birds swooped into another tree. The jay made the peculiar squawk and scream again, and the hawk shook its feathers and made small whistling noises. Instead of flying away to escape the predator, however, the jay hopped *nearer* to the small hawk, clearly daring its pursuer to chase it again. The hawk obligingly lunged at the jay, and both disappeared into the canopy to the accompaniment of raucous calls from other jays that discreetly had been watching the daredevil.

The beech woods were quiet for a few moments except for the whisper of falling hop hornbeam leaves. These small understory trees are among the first to lose their leaves, and they do so inconspicuously, as though in embarrassment. The brown or yellow leaves landed among patches of beechdrops, a wildflower that had just come up under the beech trees. Beechdrops look more like fantasies in pinkish gray plastic than flowers—they are parasitic on the beech roots and have no chlorophyll—but a close look reveals lobed petals, stamens, and pistil. Other odd-looking parasites or saprophytes also had appeared since the rain—lopsided brown mushrooms, round white ones, and others resembling orange peel.

Suddenly the sharp-shinned hawk swooped down through the canopy. This time the bluejay was chasing *it*. When the hawk landed on a branch, the jay perched just above and peered down rakishly. The hawk sat glumly with its head between its shoulders until the jay gave its peculiar scream and squawk again. At this the hawk bulleted out of the beech woods, heading south. The jay was close behind it. The other jays then burst into a fanfare of "Jay!" calls, like a bullfight crowd shouting "Ole!"

The rainy weather grew increasingly dark and cold until the autumnal equinox, after which the sky cleared and a hot spell worthy of July ensued. As though refreshed by the rain, golden-rods and asters reached new heights of brilliance and abundance. The marsh was as green and effulgent as ever. Mats of pink-flowered smartweed and tall clumps of New England aster blazed beside the still-flowering jewelweeds.

New animals had appeared in the marsh. Meadow grass-hoppers sat in sunlit silver maple saplings making stridulations that sounded like "Flick flick fleeeeeee! Flick flick fleeeee!" They were jade green insects with gray faces, red eyes, and gro-tesquely elongated hind legs and antennae, the joints and thighs of the legs bright yellow. The mats of smartweed and cutgrass swarmed with phantom crane flies, diaphanous insects whose nearly invisible legs were banded with pale blue. Until one discerned their slender bodies, the marsh seemed to be drifted over with constellations of blue dots like insubstantial life forms from some other biosphere.

But there were also signs of decline around the marsh. Silver maple leaves were touched with red, and some ash saplings in adjacent old fields had turned completely to gold and purple. In a withered maple leaf beside one of the enthusiastically stridulat-ing meadow grasshoppers, the brown chrysalis of a moth or butterfly hung upright, looking uncannily like a mummy propped against the wall of a tomb. Its rigid immobility seemed to admonish the orange question mark and yellow sulphur butterflies that still fluttered about the hot, sunny marsh.

LEAF COLOR

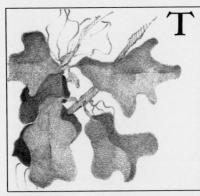

THE RIDGE'S songbird populations shifted from day to day as the migratory season advanced, the fall migrants passing through inconspicuously in their drab plumage and unmusical mood. Departed wood thrushes, blue gray gnatcatchers, and prairie warblers were followed one day by hermit thrushes, black-throated blue warblers, and yellow-rumped warblers that had nested near the Great Lakes, and on the next day by Swainson's thrushes, golden-crowned kinglets, and blackpoll warblers that had nested near Hudson Bay.

One afternoon in early October an immature magnolia warbler traversed the ridge, flying southward from weed to weed along the township road. The gray and yellow warbler had not even grown tail feathers yet and resembled a giant bumblebee as much as a bird as it flitted from tick trefoil stalk to sweet cicely stem in search of insects. Sometimes it hopped sparrowlike on the ground, sometimes it hovered before aster clumps hummingbird fashion. Its beak hung open the entire half hour it took to cover the ridge as if in continued astonishment at its own audacity in proposing to travel from Canada to Central America at its tender age.

The yellow-billed cuckoo fledgling left the ridge that evening although the night was warm and the katydids were still singing. It was not compelled by outward necessity—there were still plenty of caterpillars—but by an interaction of internal and external stimuli still too complex for human understanding. Well nourished from its rich insect diet, the cuckoo was strong enough to fly to South America. Somehow this vitality was stirred to restlessness by changes of the season—by shortening days perhaps, or cooler nights. The normally phlegmatic bird showed its restlessness by flying nervously from treetop to treetop as the sun went down and a crescent moon began to shine.

It had been restless in the evenings of preceding days, too, but the moon had not been shining so brightly. So perhaps it was the waxing moon that finally triggered a change in the young bird's orientation, a change from the familiar woods of the ridge to the mysterious sky map which steers migrating birds southward. Whatever the stimulus, the change was complete not long after the last reflected sunlight left the west and the stars came out.

The moonlit world of oak and maple fell swiftly away, and the cuckoo's field of vision became a sweep of stars and dark horizons broken here and there by the confusions of airplanes and transmission towers. As it sped south, it passed or was passed by other migrants—hummingbirds that buzzed along like bullets, streamlined flocks of shorebirds, V formations of flapping, honking geese. Later in the night its restlessness would be overcome by fatigue. It would seek a roost and spend the day resting until its emotions drove it on again, each night's flight more sustained until it was ready for the long pull across the Gulf. Then there would be the unknown but welcoming world of mahogany trees and howler monkeys and large, exotic caterpillars.

Although there were no cuckoo calls on the ridge next morning, there was much activity. Flocks of robins and chimney swifts flew over as the sky turned from dull red to peach to pink. The crows started a hysterical racket of caws as though they had suddenly discovered an owl in their midst. This seemed entirely possible, since horned owls had been calling from every clump of trees a few minutes before. The crows streamed over the hay meadow, ignoring the chill, dew-soaked grass and heading for cornfields being harvested in the lowland. They left the meadow to a pair of Carolina wrens squabbling in the honey locust.

Many trees around the meadow were showing color, although the ridge was still largely green. Shagbark hickories had turned a coarse russet color, sycamores a duller red ochre, bitternut hickories and locusts a rather nondescript yellow. The orange of sassafras was the only brilliant leaf color so far. Trees changed more quickly in full sunlight than in the woods. Most of the ash and elm saplings in the brushy places had turned or dropped their leaves, while the mature elms and ashes were still green.

The day grew warm and increasingly hazy, almost misty. Insect activity in the goldenrods and asters was still considerable but seemed to be losing momentum, perhaps because many goldenrods were going to seed. Dozens of bees frequented the asters, but beetles and bugs were less in evidence. Butterfly weed pods had split along their seams and curled back, freeing the downy seeds. The umbels of Queen Anne's lace had turned brown and withered, like charred doilies. The only old field plant not in decline was broomsedge. The heads on its purple-jointed stems were just flowering, the lemon yellow stamens dangling prettily from the spikelets.

In the hay meadow hardy timothy and clover actually grew better in the autumn coolness and still crawled with crickets and grasshoppers—big yellow grasshoppers with pink legs and smaller ones with gray, spiky bullet-heads. In the ground the box turtle eggs, laid three months before, began to hatch, the silver-dollar-size turtles tearing open the leathery shells with the egg teeth on their beaks. They were soft shelled and vulnerable, but there was no urgency to crawl out and head for water as with aquatic turtles—no crowd of predators waiting to take advantage of a frantic scramble for safety. The little box turtles could simply remain where they were—nourished by yolk sacs on their bellies—until their shells hardened and conditions became favorable. Infant box turtles are so well concealed from enemies that they are rarely seen, and their activities remain somewhat mysterious.

As the day wore on, the haze deepened into low clouds that blocked the sun. The crows returned from the cornfields and settled on the hay meadow, carrying on just as noisily as in the morning. There were more of them than in the spring, and they formed several turbulent groups, perhaps centering around pairs that had nested and their fledglings. There was much lunging at neighbors with shiny black beaks and much hopping into the air to escape from such attacks. A constant stream of arrivals and departures kept the crows stirred up, and the din of caws drowned all other sounds although it didn't appear to bother a groundhog that was eating clover a few feet from one group.

There was an even louder outburst of caws from crows hidden in the beech woods, and the groups in the meadow dispersed and fled into the trees. All the crows fell silent, and two flew into the patch of ash saplings just above the meadow. The two crows landed, looked down, then broke into caws of such giddy excitement it seemed they would have fits. They dashed for the woods at top speed and disappeared.

The other crows evidently interpreted these caws quite differently from those relating to owls, for they did not respond in kind but drifted away quietly instead. Only a few crows were still visible at the tops of the beeches when the cattle raiser emerged from the ash thicket with a sack of black walnuts he had gathered on the north slope. He crossed the meadow and walked through the beech woods, giving a fright to a pair of whitetail does and two young raccoons that had been loitering there.

The does—already in gray winter pelage—simply faded into the sassafras thickets at the bottom of the slope, but the half-grown raccoons found themselves in a predicament. Both began to climb trees; unfortunately, the trees they chose were a black cherry and a white ash that didn't branch for fifty feet or so. The raccoons had to climb this distance in plain sight of the man. They did so adeptly enough, using the bark plates as ladder rungs, but with a certain nervousness, as though unconvinced of the wisdom of their escape routes. Eventually they reached the treetops and disappeared into the foliage.

The cattle raiser walked to the foot of the slope and stood quietly in a clump of sassafras. Five minutes elapsed, then one of the raccoons emerged from the canopy, crept headfirst down the trunk quite silently, and scrambled away downhill. Another ten minutes passed, then the second raccoon started down its tree. Unlike its bolder sibling, it was clearly worried about the man standing nearby and kept pausing in its gingerly descent to peer at him, its small black mask very alert and concerned. When it reached the ground, it scampered uphill instead of down. The cattle raiser smiled and went home.

This smile represents an enigma to the modern mind, with its preference for drawing clear ethical boundaries to matters of life and death. It was an affectionate smile, yet the cattle raiser and his dogs probably would kill several raccoons during the hunting season. Such affection for an object of destruction may seem perverse in a milieu where actions imply choices between right and wrong. It may inspire something of the missionary's confused alarm upon being confronted with an aboriginal tribe whose mores include both great generosity and headhunting. In fact, affection for prey probably *is* an aboriginal human trait if the association of hominid fossils and cracked antelope bones is to be credited. It's doubtful the great cave art of the Pleistocene could have been created without love for the red deer and aurochs the artists sought to "capture."

Today this love is more often expressed in decals on camper-trailers than in great art, but it exists beside and often entangled with more civilized modes of affection for wildlife that originated from it. To be successful, the most pacific birdwatcher must have something of the old desire to track, stalk, and capture quarry, since birds don't discriminate clearly between watchers and hunters. The cattle raiser's smile had much in common with the smile on some archaic statues, a smile that puzzles restless museum-goers with its untroubled acquiescence to life on earth. It also had something in common with the "smile" sometimes seen on the faces of hunting wolves and coyotes—an expression of pleasure that has been distorted by fabulists into the slinking grin of the outlaw, but that is older than laws, predating guilt and innocence.

LATE BREEDERS

Low, misty clouds caused an extravagant sunset that evening. The red sun sank like a burning boat into a gray sea of cumulus clouds above the western horizon, its pink rays slanting through ragged white mist below the clouds. This mist drifted southward as the sun sank behind the clouds, leaving a violet gulf at the horizon into which the sun reappeared when it descended below the cumulus layer. By that time it was no longer red, as if the sea of clouds had put out its fires. A gentle rain began to fall, bringing satisfied clucks from worm-hunting robins. Mourning doves rocketed overhead, and crows flew back and forth excitedly, perhaps wondering what the cattle raiser had been up to with the sack.

A horned owl called from the woods, and rain began to fall hard, although the deep blue sky was only partly obscured by misty clouds. When the sun sank below the horizon, a suffusion of brilliant rosy light spread across the eastern sky, turning the trees into ultramarine blue silhouettes. The meadow was electric green in this light, which seemed more a primary source of illumination than a reflection of the sun's last rays from airborne water droplets. The strange brilliance appeared and faded in the time it took to walk across the meadow, then the trees that had been silhouetted against it began to glow with warm, saturated tones of their own—greenish ochres and umbers reminiscent of seventeenth-century Dutch landscapes. Soon this glow faded, too, and the clouds darkened. A warm breeze began to blow, scattering yellow ash leaves across the meadow. Crickets began to sing.

The warm, wet night was very much like the late winter night that had brought the spotted salamanders out to breed. It didn't seem to affect them—even the few larvae that had survived the summer had left the oxbow and spring pool and gone underground. The October night had a message for a very different group of salamanders—the woodland salamanders of the genus *Plethodon*. These are slender, usually drab-colored amphibians that spend their entire lives on land, not even going into the water to breed. Oddly, considering their terrestrial habits, they don't have lungs, organs that the water-breeding spotted salamanders do have. They get their oxygen by diffusion through the skin.

When it was quite dark, thousands of red-backed salamanders crawled from daytime retreats under logs and stones and climbed twigs, rocks, and other objects that projected above the leaf litter. One could have walked the entire extent of the ridge's mature woods trampling a red-backed salamander with each step. Some of them climbed the quarry walls and clung vertically like lizards. They were delicate little batrachians with large, lustrous eyes, slate gray flanks, and speckled bellies. Some had reddish brown stripes down their backs, others were plain gray, but all belonged to the same species. None was more than five inches long, tail included.

Rainy nights in spring and summer would bring out many red-backed salamanders to hunt for insects (and fall prey to the many predators that found them a reliable food supply), but never this many. Now was the beginning of their breeding season, and they were answering the same mysterious call the spotted salamanders had answered a half year before.

When each salamander reached the top of its twig or stone, it paused there like a statue. The woods became a salamander sculpture gallery. This urge to climb objects was perhaps a way of bringing the sexes together, since there were only so many sticks and rocks and the chances of two salamanders meeting on one were statistically increased. In fact, some of the twigs and rocks were occupied by two individuals. Male red-backed salamanders possess hedonic glands with scent secretions attractive to females. These glands are much more extensive than those of the spotted salamander, reflecting the inferiority of air as a transporting medium for perfumes.

None of the pedestaled salamanders were mating yet. They would retire to safety underground for that. A male would rub the hedonic glands on his cheeks and jaw against a female's head, which would stimulate the female to press her snout against other glands at the base of his tail. The pair would then engage in a head-to-tail promenade, the male bending his tail around the female to keep her involved until he was ready to deposit his spermatophore on a leaf or twig. The excited female would pick it up with the lips of her cloaca, but instead of fertilizing her eggs within a few days, the sperm would be stored in folds of her flesh until the next summer. Then the female would lay teardroplike clusters of eggs on the undersides of rocks; and the embryos would pass through their larval stage inside the eggs, to emerge in late summer as tiny but exact replicas of their parents.

There was proof of this delayed egglaying in the woods on this night because some of the salamanders in the sculpture gallery were less than an inch long. It seemed doubtful that they could be ready to mate at such a small size, but they posed on their twigs anyway, like children playing doctor. One tiny salamander stood peaceably beside a camel cricket twice its length.

There were a great many of these hump-backed crickets around, but they did not stridulate since they had no wings. The woods were quieter than they had been for many months. A few tree crickets shrilled languidly, and earthworms still disturbed the sodden leaf litter; but the katydids were silent, and harvestmen were largely absent. Small, silvery noctuid moths fluttered about, and there were squeaks and bumps as the latest generation of white-footed mice explored the ridge, but the main sounds were the wind in the trees and the drip of water.

The red-backed salamanders weren't the only ones answering the call of the warm rain. A handsome black salamander speckled with silvery blotches crawled sedately out of a deep crevice at the base of the quarry cliff and walked downhill in search of a mate. Similar in shape to the red-backs, it was larger, over seven inches long. It was a slimy salamander, the unattractive common name of which refers to a glutinous mucus exuded by the species' skin.

Slimy salamanders belong to the same genus as red-backed salamanders and have similar breeding habits, but they need more moisture. The ridge's slimy salamander population was thus confined to deep crevices in the sandstone and was much smaller than the red-back population. There were enough to keep the species going, though, and the seven-inch individual encountered a slightly smaller slimy salamander within a few feet of its crevice. They passed each other without a glance. Perhaps they were of the same sex; it's difficult to tell with salamanders.

The short-tailed shrew had weaned her new litter, and they came out to forage in the moist darkness. The young shrews were not used to rain, and when the wind shook loose a shower of drops on them, they panicked. Each grabbed the nearest warm, furry object—the mother in two cases and the preceding sibling in the other four—and held on. The mother was not disturbed by the shower, so they kept moving along as a kind of shrew train after thus linking up. If someone had picked up the mother, the young shrews would have hung on even as they dangled in midair.

The shrew train very soon encountered a red-backed salamander, which made no effort to escape until the mother touched its tail. Then the salamander wriggled away vigorously with the shrew train in earnest pursuit. One of the young shrews was pulled loose and set up a twitter of alarm, but by this time the salamander had been captured and the shrew train had uncoupled to devour it. This was completed swiftly. The somewhat reassured young shrews did not link up again but remained in a close pack as the mother moved on after more food. They filled their stomachs without difficulty that night.

THE CANOPY TURNS

The mild weather lasted a few more days, but in the second week of October night temperatures began to fall into the low thirties with regularity. Horned owl calls became the only evening sounds on the ridge. A few kinglets and yellow-rumped warblers lingered in the abandoned orchards, but other warm weather migrants had departed. Juncos and white-throated sparrows appeared along the overgrown fencerows, and swamp sparrows again skulked in the marsh. The flocks of nighthawks and chimney swifts gave way to southward bound flocks of turkey vultures.

A flock of at least thirty-five vultures wheeled over the ridge one warm afternoon, playing on the rising air currents that marked the confluence of plateau and lowland. Many soared quite low over the ridgetop, rocking back and forth on their great wings, so low that their bright black eyes were clearly visible. The dark, ragged forms of the vultures seemed different en masse from the lazily circling individuals of hot summer days—less dispassionate, more playful and wistful, as though the hazy reaches of autumn awoke disquiet and longing in vultures as they do in humans. The crows were having a raucous gathering in the hay meadow as the vultures circled, so the ridgetop was a lively place for a little while, until the vultures drifted southward and the crows sought other diversions.

The forest canopy that the soaring vultures saw was an increasingly colorful one. The mature ashes had turned their corroded bronze colors, and fiery patches were appearing on the sun-dried tops of the other canopy trees: dark red for black and red oak; violet for white oak; scarlet for red maple and scarlet oak; green gold for beech; red gold for sugar maple; red yellow for black cherry. Abscission layers had formed at the leaf stem bases, cutting off the flow of sugars from the leaves' photosynthetic cells. Chlorophyll faded from the leaves, revealing the yellow carotenoids and red anthocyanins that the green pigment had masked during the growing season.

There were already bare spots in the canopy. Most of the elms, hackberries, bitternut hickories, sycamores, and black walnuts had already dropped their leaves. Brushy places were largely leafless, their brownish violet color now in strong contrast to the still-green mature woods when the ridge was seen from the lowland. Around the marsh silver maples and willows were still leafy and green, but other wetland plants had changed abruptly because of the low night temperatures.

The jewelweed simply seemed to have vanished, until one noticed a meager litter of shriveled, rotten stems and leaves on the ground. It was incredible that plants that had taken up so much space in life could be reduced so quickly, but the succulent jewelweeds were mostly water and had collapsed into pulp when frozen. The cattail leaves still stood thickly, but they had turned brown, and something had trampled them at the bottom of the marsh. The trampling revealed many crayfish chimneys— mud parapets that the crustaceans pile up at their burrow entrances—and a profuse litter of raccoon droppings. On the upper reaches of the marsh the mat of cutgrass and smartweed also was turning brown. The few water plantains and water

hemlocks in the spring pool had disappeared, as had most of the green algae.

The goldenrods in the old fields faded to khaki color except for the silky white bristles of their seed heads. Pale beige milkweed pods split open and released hundreds of mahogany seeds, each with its white plume of down. The plumed seeds drifted on the breeze past breeding swarms of midges, insects and seeds alternately glittering and fading from sight as they passed through the rays of the late afternoon sun. Asters were still flowering, still covered with bees on warm afternoons, but the insects disappeared swiftly in the evening shadows.

A few tree crickets called hesitantly in early evening, and noctuid moths fluttered against the darkening sky, but the colorful moths of summer were gone, as were the bizarre micrathena spiders. The diminution of insect songs and thinning of vegetation brought the surrounding world of electric light and mechanical noise closer than it had been for months. The ridge seemed to shrink, and this was more than a mere impression, since the biomass of the insects, spiders, birds, leaves, flowers, and other living things that now were dying or departing must have weighed in the tons. The first heavy frost came soon after the middle of October. Atmospheric moisture precipitated as ice crystals instead of dew; and the meadow, pastures, and old fields were sparkling white in the morning. The spring pool steamed like a kettle. In the woods many foot-long leaves of pawpaw had fallen overnight. They hadn't changed color but had merely turned dry and papery; they lay on the leaf litter like heaps of silvery green fish. An aching silence lasted until sunlight had evaporated the hoarfrost, then the ridge began to stir again. Except for the pawpaws, the ridge seemed little the worse for the frost. Grass was still growing, and the brushlands were full of the green spikes of wild chives that had come up since the nights turned cold, and that would persist until spring.

The woods filled up with chipmunks in the afternoon, especially the south slope beech woods, which had produced a good nut crop. Groundhogs, squirrels, jays, robins, flickers, and red-headed woodpeckers also favored the beechnuts, and the autumn grove was like a bank on payday—a gold-lit, silver-pillared hall full of well-fed noises. Toward evening a huge crow flock—several hundred birds—landed in the beech tops with the usual commotion and was joined by a much larger grackle flock whose cries drowned out even the crows. Then, following some obscure collective impulse, both flocks took wing at once—another everyday mystery. The grackles flew east, the crows west.

In the ensuing quiet a crackling came from a blackberry bush at the bottom of the slope. One of the small raccoons emerged, climbed halfway up a leaning tree, then returned to the briar patch. The small raccoon reentered the briar patch, emerged again, climbed halfway up the same tree again, then disappeared a final time. Perhaps it was restless to begin the night's feeding, or perhaps the small raccoon's oddly repetitive behavior did not have any such rational explanation. Animals are generally more purposeful in their actions than they seem to casual observation, but the purposes are not always easy to understand. The most familiar animals, such as raccoons, may be the hardest, since so much of their behavior is adapted to furtive survival in a human-dominated world.

Just before dark fifty crows began circling the marsh. One by one they sideslipped and dropped down into the silver maple saplings where they were visible hopping about rather clumsily. They seemed prepared to roost, which was unusual—crows had not roosted anywhere on the ridge that year. They might have had some protection from the No Hunting signs on the park property, but human laws mean nothing to crows. They have their own requirements, even more inscrutable than a raccoon's. Crows are so difficult to comprehend that even the great ethologist Konrad Lorenz seems to have despaired of studying them. He found that it was "apparently unbelievably difficult to rear healthy crows," and so was unable to observe a tame flock as he did with jackdaws and geese. On Chestnut Ridge it was surprising how little crows revealed of their motives and movements. They were usually present, cawing above the treetops; but when attention was focused on them, they would drift away giving no indication of where they were going or where they had come from. So it was with the flock in the silver maples. The crows seemed to change their minds after a few minutes and moved back westward over the ridgetop in scattered, softly-calling groups. Sparks of red sunset gleamed on inky feathers as they streamed through the woods.

For a few days the frosty mornings warmed into crisp afternoons with the curiously deep blue skies that appear only in autumn. Leaf color spread swiftly to the lower branches in the woods. Beeches darkened from topaz to amber, and the translucent leaves of sugar maples cast a brilliant auburn light on the ground. The east slope woods did not glow as brightly as the south or west slopes since the oak leaves that predominated in its canopy were more opaque than the beech or maple leaves. But the oaks' ranges of violet, maroon, scarlet, and crimson had a resonance that deepened the more one looked at them. This subtlety was typical of the oaks. They were rarely the first trees one admired, but their clean lines grew in attraction as do the features of people who seem plain at first but have an exceptional grace and symmetry of bone structure.

The asters went to seed, and the old fields were plain brown again. Crickets still hopped around, though, and bees visited a last few flower heads. On a faded Queen Anne's lace leaf, a black swallowtail butterfly larva stopped eating. It had grown in the past month from a diminutive black and white worm into a black-banded, yellow-spotted, green caterpillar three inches long. The green color indicated that it was ready to pupate. It spent a day hanging from the leaf in a hunched position, apparently idle, but its pupal case was forming rapidly under the caterpillar skin. By the next afternoon a spiky green chrysalis hung on a strong loop of silk where the larva had been. A small wad of shed skin on the ground was all that remained of the handsome caterpillar.

THE CANOPY FALLS

The old box turtle had found a hibernaculum, but he still emerged from it on warm afternoons. Turtles sometimes come out to bask in mid-January if the weather is warm, although they may be trapped by sudden temperature drops and freeze to death. The box turtle found less to eat, but he was not much interested in food anyway. He did eat a few mushrooms, for which box turtles have a decided taste, apparently being immune to poisonous kinds, which makes box turtles a dubious ingredient in turtle soup. Mostly he just sat in the sun, perhaps reponding to the richness of color around him. Turtles are known to see colors, so why shouldn't they enjoy them?

Then a bitter cold rain began, and the turtle crawled deep into the ground. The oak and beech leaves faded to various shades of brown, and the auburn of maple turned a bright but somehow lifeless butter yellow. Heavy with rain, the leaves did not spin or drift as they fell but dropped and lay in sodden heaps—oak and beech leaves stiff and slimy like old linoleum, maple leaves floppy and mushy like uneaten cornflakes, silver maple and willow leaves crumpled and glutinous like used tissue paper. Dogwood and red maple leaves kept their bright color even on the ground, but this didn't interrupt the overall drab impression. From a distance the ridge was violet gray except for threadbare patches of brown or yellow canopy.

There were exceptions to the general decline. Some black cherry and slippery elm saplings had simply refused to turn. They remained green and nearly full-leaved, perhaps from some genetic distortion of the chemical messages that normally destroy leaf chloroplasts. These trees looked very inappropriate in the damp gray brush. As though to compound the anomaly, the big female raccoon was climbing around in one leafy cherry tree. Despite the bone-chilling rain, she sprawled upside down and nonchalantly gobbled the tree's somewhat shriveled fruits as though it were an August afternoon. Her behavior may have been related to the alcohol content of the rotting cherries. Robins regularly get drunk and disorderly when the black cherry crop is overripe. Perhaps the raccoon was celebrating her liberation from motherhood.

The short-tailed shrew and her brood suddenly experienced a scarcity of food. They hurried around their tunnels eating the few comatose insects and spiders they could find, then ventured onto the forest floor, where they found even less. They ate some fruits and seeds, but the brushy ridgetop was not as rich in such foods as the mature woods. If they had lived in the beech woods, they would have been better off, but it was well beyond their small range.

They burrowed in the humus and leaf litter, but it was so sodden and cold that one young shrew was soaked and died of hypothermia. Another died of starvation and was eaten by its siblings, three of which used the strength thus acquired to disperse in search of food, never to return. The other remained with its mother. There was hardly enough food in the area even for two shrews—now that the cold weather had depleted invertebrate populations—but the last infant was too timid to leave familiar surroundings. The mother shrew remained because she was exhausted from raising the brood. The two moved listlessly around the impoverished tunnels, finding enough food to stay alive but not to stay healthy.

In early November a short reprieve arrived. A south wind began to blow and the weather warmed. Crickets crawled out of sheltered niches and hopped and chirped as if it were still September. Water striders skated on creek pools that had been rimmed with ice a day before. Even the nights were warm, and the short-tailed shrews were able to find camel crickets and earthworms. Surprisingly, a few cone-headed grasshoppers and tree crickets began calling, and the twilights were again full of midges and noctuid moths.

There was really nothing to be surprised about in the resurgence of insects on the November ridge, though. No group in the animal kingdom rivals the resilience of insects—their ability to outlive or outbreed the most adverse environmental factors and swiftly take advantage of favorable ones. Insect populations function in a world of exponential growth that is not really accessible to vertebrate humans, no matter how crowded and antlike our own population becomes. Even the limited insect world of a year on Chestnut Ridge is beyond comprehension. An army of entomologists could not count and identify all the insects that inhabit Chestnut Ridge in one year, much less understand their ecology. Even if they could, they still would not be able to predict exactly what the next year's insect generations would do.

Insect populations remain a step ahead of human understanding and control because they are more complex and multifarious than the human brain; more "intelligent," in a sense. This complexity eventually "outwits" attempts to "solve the insect problem" because it is so much subtler than the solutions. Agribusiness is taught this lesson many times a year (as the old apple farmer of Chestnut Ridge may have been taught it after climbing on the pesticide treadmill), but the lesson is perhaps too simple to be learned. A computer big enough to understand and predict insect population behavior might be built, but this seems unlikely given the probability that the majority of insect species haven't even been named yet. For the present, civilization is out of its depth in trying to master insects and fortunate in still having spiders, shrews, and songbirds to buffer their genuinely explosive populations. A man-insect planet would be a last frontier on which the bones of more than a few pioneers would bleach.

A pair of red bats on migration frequented the ridge on these warm evenings. The orange-furred bats used the sparsely trafficked township road as a flyway, fluttering back and forth along it to scoop up moths and midges that emerged from the woods. It was easier than chasing them through the trees. Walkers on the road found it a little disconcerting to see bats suddenly flying up the road directly at their heads, but the little mammals always hedgehopped over just in time, often close enough to stir the hair with their wings. The bats spent the days hanging from buckeye trees in the woods, where they resembled dead leaves until one drew close enough to see the tiny snouts between their folded wings. Sometimes they yawned, baring extraordinary mouthfuls of teeth.

The woods were full of nut-gathering birds and mammals while the warmth lasted, particularly the north slope where birds found shelter from the often boisterous south wind. Flickers and a pair of pileated woodpeckers hopped on fallen logs, pulling the punky wood apart effortlessly to get at grubs and ants. The jay-size flickers looked puny compared to the red-crested, black and white pileated woodpeckers, which are as large as crows.

The south wind blew down most of the beech, maple, and oak leaves; and when the weather turned cold again, the winter aspect of the ridge was suddenly complete. The quarries looked naked without their leaf canopy: the green shade had made them inviting and mysterious, like caves, but now they were simply rock outcroppings. The dampish smell of humus and a faint, dusty odor of impending snow replaced the redolence of green vegetation. The latest trash dumpings were conspicuous along the township road now that the underbrush was bare. Everything imaginable was dumped—live kittens, major appliances, whole rooms of furniture. This time someone appeared to have cleaned out an office; there were bills and canceled checks with the presumed dumper's name and address, as though to flaunt defiance of antilitter ordinances. The retired contractor and his dog came ambling along the road one evening as a group was unloading an unwanted hot water heater and kitchen sink in the woods. He expressed an opinion about their activity, had a shotgun waved at him for his pains, and went home in all earnestness to get his own gun. The dumpers had departed when he returned to the woods, though, so he relieved his feelings by shooting several holes in the water heater.

146

The old fields did not assume the stark aspect of the woods; they merely lost their color. Red gold leaves and silky white seed bristles of broomsedge were the only bright things in them. The pastures had faded to yellow, but the stock raiser hadn't taken the steers off them yet. He brought them hay instead. The southerly exposed hay meadow was still green, though, and the crows still settled on it in the afternoon when they returned from eating corn in the lowlands.

HARD FROST

THE FALL of the woodland canopy was a dramatic emblem of summer's end, but the melancholy aspect of the spectacle was somewhat misleading. The fallen leaves were not the last leaves of the summer; they were the last leaves of the previous summer. The leaves of the summer just passed were still on the trees, tenderly wrapped in winter buds located above the scars of the fallen leaves' stems. Formed inconspicuously during the summer growing season, the buds concealed tiny leaves, twigs, or flowers that required only a dormant period and a rush of spring sap to unfold and recreate the canopy within a few days.

Each tree species had winter buds as distinctive as its leaves. Oak buds were stout and many-scaled like tiny pine cones. Beech buds were slender and graceful—golden ornaments tipping the silver branches. Bitternut hickory buds were sulfur yellow and flame-shaped.

The buds seemed fragile containers to protect the trees' reproductive and food-making tissues through the winter, but their waxy scales helped to keep the new leaves and flowers from freezing even when they were ice covered. Most of the plants on the ridge folded their soft tissues into some such miniaturized form for the winter. Woody shrubs and vines carried buds on their stems and branches, as did trees. Grasses and perennial or biennial herbs such as milkweed and goldenrod budded from the rootstock or from underground stems. Jewelweed and other annual plants depended on seeds, tough coats enclosing embryonic plants and their food supplies. Even the winter green herbs —avens, crowfoot, violets—depended on buds for the next growing season's leaves and flowers. The winter green leaves were evolutionary afterthoughts and looked it. They were wilted and tattered—tenacious but expendable.

The true evergreens on the ridge were the primitive plants that lived in odd corners of the deciduous forest. There were green scums of filamentous algae on beech trunks; mats of haircap and cushion moss on the woodland floor; tufts of Christmas fern on quarry walls; sprigs of ebony spleenwort and running ground pine in the scrubland. There were a few red cedar trees too large to have been stolen for lawn shrubbery by neighboring suburbanites. These plants remained stoically and tidily green through the coldest weather as though hurrying to catch up by their thrifty but clumsy photosynthesizing with the more sophisticated angiosperms that sprawled above them, untidy in their winter sleep.

Many of the ridge's animals used miniaturization strategies similar to the angiosperms' for surviving the winter. The insect pupae on virtually every square foot of the ridge were similar in function to the plant buds, protecting delicate tissues until the time was right for their emergence. One box elder sapling near the marsh was hung with so many bagworm moth cocoons that they might indeed have been its buds. The bagworm caterpillars had festooned their gray silk cocoons with box elder leaf stems, so the cocoons looked as much vegetable in origin as animal.

But it is unsafe to draw any but general analogies between plants and animals. The mobility of animals has led them into a maze of evolutionary adaptation that makes the plants seem simple and straightforward. The bagworm cocoons beside the marsh did not really contain pupae, but eggs. The blind, legless female bagworms had pupated and reached adulthood in early autumn without ever growing wings or leaving their cocoons. They only left their cocoons after the black, winged males had mated with them and they had laid their masses of white eggs in the cocoons. Then they crawled out, fell to the ground, and were eaten by ants and birds.

The bagworm eggs would remain in the cocoons until the

spring, when the young caterpillars would crawl out and begin eating box elder leaves. It was as though one opened the winter buds of some tree and found already germinating seeds instead of next year's miniaturized flowers. Nor did the animals' evolutionary deviousness end there. Some of the bagworm eggs contained other eggs—the embryos of small wasps that parasitize moth eggs.

There were many such unpredictabilities among the ridge's animal populations. Spider egg cases that dangled from abandoned webs were likely to contain not eggs but hatched spiderlings that would spend the winter feeding on one another, the well-nourished survivors to emerge when warm weather returned. The young of other spider species left the egg sac in autumn and scattered to spend the winter in sheltered spots. The year's crop of green frog tadpoles had not turned into adults and crawled into the mud to hibernate as had the toads and spotted salamanders. For some reason it took them two years to mature, so they spent the winter swimming under the ice; and many died from starvation or suffocation.

Reptiles and birds were more straightforward than invertebrates and amphibians. They had sensibly laid their eggs (or had borne their young live in the case of garter and water snakes) in the spring or summer; and the eggs had hatched in time for the young to migrate, find shelter, or grow strong enough to endure the winter. With the mammals, however, things grew somewhat complicated again. Two big brown bat females hibernating in a deep quarry crevice were using the same reproductive strategy as the red-backed and slimy salamanders. They had mated in October, but were not pregnant: the sperm was stored in their uteruses and would not be used until the eggs were shed from the ovaries in spring. Other mammals were pregnant and would bear or carry their young in this bleakest time of year. Meadow mice mate throughout the year, so there were always a few pregnant mice on the ridge; and a pregnant doe had taken up residence.

The doe and her two lanky fawns from the summer moved onto the ridge in mid-November, appearing beside the marsh very early one clear, cold morning. A sound like someone trying to start a power lawnmower came from the silver maple thickets

—the two fawns were chasing each other about the marsh pools, their sharp hooves clattering on the frozen vegetation. The doe stood off to one side and paid no attention to this nonsense. She browsed a few willow buds, but grew uneasy as the sky paled. The marsh didn't offer enough cover to please her.

The sun came up through a notch in the southeast hills, its rays sparkling on the hoarfrost as though the dead cutgrass and smartweeds were covered with red, green, and blue diamonds. Clouds of steam from the gamboling fawns' mouths turned pearly white in the sun's light, but they stopped playing soon after it rose. Their mother had begun moving away up the south slope, and they hurried after her. She was less solicitous of them than during the summer and had lost interest in them completely while a buck had courted her a few days before. But they would stay with her as long as they could. She represented stability in a very confusing environment.

A gang of crows flew into the beeches as the sun rose higher. They saw the deer moving up from the marsh, but they were more interested in the hay meadow, where the cattle raiser had just driven his pickup and was unloading a chain saw. The crows cocked their heads at him and flew stealthily from tree to tree, obviously up to something. They had been getting ready to mob a young horned owl, but now they waited silently instead. The man left his truck and approached the woods.

As soon as the cattle raiser passed through the blackberry thicket at the meadow edge and entered the trees, an explosion of caws forced the owl to flee its perch. It was in full view of the man for several seconds as it flapped away with talons dangling, long enough for a clear shot if the chain saw had been a gun. A few crows also were visible through the treetops, but the black birds had succeeded, as neatly as if they had planned it, in exposing the owl to the man while showing little of themselves. If the cattle raiser had been a poacher, they would have been rid of one of their demons.

The cawing stopped promptly when the owl disappeared, and there was some confused flying back and forth as though to investigate the owl's disappointing escape. The crows kept well up in the trees, however—that the man did not shoot the owl was no guarantee he wouldn't shoot crows. One of the red-tailed hawks appeared in curiosity and was chased and dived at for its interest. Then the cattle raiser started his chain saw and began to cut up the red oak that had fallen during the summer. The woods emptied of birds as the raucous snarl arose, and the doe and her fawns sneaked away into the west slope gullies.

At noon the cattle raiser drove away with his truckload of fire-wood, and the beech woods returned to itself. A Carolina wren sang, a chickadee squabbled with a junco, and chipmunks made a surprising amount of noise in the dry fallen beech leaves. A large bald-faced hornet's nest was conspicuous in the treetops after being hidden by the leaf canopy all summer. Tenanted only this one year, the gray, papery sphere was full of dead workers and pupae. It would hang there until a strong wind blew it down.

The noonday warmth was brief, though. The day grew chill and overcast soon after the sun passed zenith. The chipmunks disappeared with the sunlight, and the shadows that fell across the hay meadow were cold. The meadow grass was still green, but the blades and stems had a static, wilted look. They had stopped growing, although the frosts had not yet killed them. Mounds of fresh red earth newly decayed from the parent sand-stone lay at the entrance of the groundhog burrows, evidence of the preparation of groundhog winter beds. No groundhogs appeared during the afternoon—they were already hibernating.

Just before sunset one of the huge blackbird flocks of late autumn passed southward over the ridge. It was not an un-broken stream of birds, but it still took about a half hour for the loosely connected groups to fly over. The sustained rattle of calls and soughing of wings as the grackles, red-wings, starlings, and cowbirds streamed past had an effect on the observer similar to that of sitting beside a river. There was a similar urge to follow the flow, to drift away from the bounds of self-consciousness into the more fluid awareness of wild things, for whom the past flows into the future without hope or fear.

A breeze sprang up at twilight and hurried ranks of fallen leaves across the meadow or flung them upward in eddies. The leaves seemed alive, like the robins that chase each other over lawns and spring into the air to beat one another with their wings. These leaf flocks were nearly silent, though; there were only slight rustlings and whisperings as they jostled together.

The only other sound in the meadow was the wind in the tree-tops.

A month before, the wind had roared and boomed in the leaf canopy, but now it only clicked and whistled. The stars were brilliant above the bare branches, and their light—reaching the forest floor for the first time in months—made the leaf litter seem strangely smooth and shiny, like a black and polished dance floor. Not everything had changed, however. An opossum that had been climbing the south slope at dark since summer did so now, apparently unconcerned by the icy wind. It moved with flat-footed aplomb, pausing several times to sniff and listen before disappearing into ridgetop thickets.

EARLY SNOWFALL

The first snow came a little before Thanksgiving, a damp snow that lasted only long enough to record a dawn of animal activity. The doe and her fawns left the shapes of their bodies and yellow spots of urine where they had bedded in a gully, and the ridgetop was crisscrossed with rabbit tracks. This was a little surprising since the cottontails had seemed scarce since the summer's end, when they had stopped coming out of the brush to eat clover. A network of fox squirrel tracks in the woods also belied an apparent scarcity of the big, quiet squirrels with their hand-some orange bellies. The bearlike tracks of raccoons, the splay-toed tracks of opossums, and the neat, doglike tracks of foxes meandered all over the ridge.

When the snow melted, it uncovered the corpse of the short-tailed shrew. She lay on her side on the ridgetop path, open jaws revealing her tiny pink tongue and yellow teeth. The red pigment that had tipped them when she was young was worn away, and the teeth were blunted by use. Her fur was a little matted by the wet snow; otherwise there was no mark of disturbance on her, no blood.

Shrews are often found dead in this way, especially in late autumn. She had emerged from her tunnels during the night—perhaps drawn by some memory of youthful pleasure in the snow—and a shock had overstressed a metabolism weakened by fatigue and poor nutrition. The shock might have been as inconsequential as a falling branch, but the grain-size heart had spasmed and stopped. Her body lay in the path for two days, preserved by the cold, then it was gone overnight.

The weather turned warm for a few days after the snow, but there was little response to the warmth. Crickets and grasshoppers remained silent. A few flies and honeybees buzzed about; a few ants and wolf spiders hurried through the old fields; a few yellow-rumped warblers and ruby-crowned kinglets foraged in the orchards. Bird calls were at a minimum: as long as the days kept getting shorter, the resident songbirds were interested only in finding food and avoiding cold winds. The somber aspect of the ridge seemed anomalous in the gentle weather. One half expected the plants to start leafing out, but they remained obstinately bare and gray. Only the bright amber of broomsedge seemed in harmony with the pink and azure sunsets that ended these days.

On the morning when the weather turned cold again, a pair of half-grown red foxes bounded across the township road and climbed the ridge. They were following a trail much used by foxes, although they didn't know where they were going. Their parents had driven them away from their den in the pasture lands to the west, and they were wandering, mercifully unaware that their chances of surviving the winter as transients were small.

A variety of deaths awaited the little foxes. They might be run over on one of the many roads they would cross. Roads are often littered with mangled young foxes around Thanksgiving time. There was a good chance that dogs would kill them or that they would die of distemper, a disease perennially renewed in the countryside by abandonment or neglect of dogs and cats. Rabies was a less likely but real possibility—a much crueler death than the preceding. They might be caught in leghold traps, a death requiring a few hours if the trapper was conscientious and checked his line every morning, a few days if he was not. If they were lucky enough to avoid these human-influenced dangers, there were always the old deaths of hunger or accidental injury. Although they had no way of anticipating these dangers, their aloneness frightened them and they moved along with a great deal of nervous energy. If they could cover enough ground, they might come to a place where they would be safe for a while, where there was food, cover, and not too many people or foxes.

The ridge was not the place for them, however. It was too heavily wooded, too much hunted over by the gray foxes that denned there. Red foxes need expanses of open country—there had not been red foxes for hundreds of miles around the ridge before white settlers removed the forest. The little foxes trotted through the black locust saplings smelling old spoors of rabbit, mouse, shrew, and opossum, but found nothing worth further investigation. They hunted mainly at night and now felt an urge to run, to cover ground before the day became too advanced and they had to seek cover. They crossed the ridgetop without pausing and raced through the east slope woods, then moved more cautiously through the old fields below until they had safely crossed the county road, skirted a house (with a sudden barking of kenneled dogs), and moved into northeastern cornfields. They were gangly, scruffy little foxes, but tireless runners.

The next snow came one afternoon in early December, falling not in wet clots but in pellets like tiny hailstones that bounced and rattled on the leaf litter. The pellets fell so thickly that they deadened other sounds. The woods were hushed, full of whispers. Traffic was still audible from the county road, but it didn't penetrate. It was like distant thunder, a passing disturbance.

In a little while the snow pellets became softer, settling on the fallen leaves instead of bouncing. They became the elaborate crystalline doilies of snowflakes, some quite large, their symmetrical patterning visible without magnification. The whispering became even fainter, and the darkness of trees and honeysuckle tangles faded behind the snow, which fell at a slant although it did not seem wind driven. It seemed rather to have its own momentum, as though it were flowing in from the west instead of falling from the sky. This was true in a way because the flow of moist air and dust particles on which the snow crystals precipitated came from the west, including the particles of hydrocarbons, heavy metals, and sulfur oxides that make the whiteness of snow less than innocent today.

A half inch of snow had fallen on the ridge by evening, and it kept falling so thickly that there was no sunset. There were only a few moments of luminosity as a ray of sunlight broke through the thin clouds at the horizon and reflected from the clouds over the ridge. It became pitch dark very quickly. Not even the horned owls called.

A two-inch blanket had accumulated by morning. It was almost unmarred by tracks, the thickness of the fall seeming to have discouraged animal activity. The snowfall stopped by sunrise, however, and juncos and white-throated sparrows marked the blanket soon enough as they scratched for seeds. Birds were conspicuous against the whiteness. A Carolina wren ate poison ivy berries while a goldfinch pecked at a bud further down the same plant. The high twittering of a tree sparrow flock came from the old fields. A bluejay rocketed out of the trees above the spring pool and landed for a drink, keeping a wary eye cocked at the same time it tipped its head back to let the water run down its throat. Then it reascended and screeched loudly, once more feeling safe in the treetops. A few faint caws carried from western cornfields, but there were no crows on the snowy ridge.

Winter was beginning earlier than the previous year, but the temperature rose into the forties again, and the snow dissolved in a soft rain. The creeks ran high and fast, and the redbelly dace, green frog tadpoles, and crayfish had to struggle against the current. It brought them food and oxygen that would be scarce later on, however. Life would become difficult in the creeks when ice covered them and their flow dwindled. It seemed unlikely that hundreds of dace could survive through the winter in creeks no more than three feet wide and a foot deep, but the schools of minnows would somehow reappear after the spring floods tore silt-darkened cakes of ice from the creek beds and scoured out new sandbars, riffles, and pools.

It wasn't only the life of the creeks that seemed unlikely in the December rain. The whole bare-branched, leaf-littered ridge sometimes resembled a pile of sticks and mud brushed into a corner more than a functioning ecosystem. It had an unfinished aspect: there was none of the exquisite tidiness of winter ever-green forests. It was more like a compost heap, an apt analogy because the drab untidiness masked a ferment rich in possibilities. Constantly playing between the poles of arctic winters and tropical summers, there is no biome more dynamic and resilient than the temperate deciduous forest, as is demonstrated by its ability—so far—to absorb the damages that humans, glaciers, and other geological forces have inflicted on it.

Indeed, the "temperate" forest's resilience is largely attributable to the extremes of climate to which it is adapted. Its wealth is in its ambiguity, in its vacillation between the cold that results in permafrost-locked soil in the north and the heat that results in humus-poor, lateritic soils in the south. The temperate forest creates humus in the warm seasons and conserves it during the cold, so humus accumulates into the rich organic soil that permits successful agriculture where geological conditions are favorable or that grows a new forest over gullied, cutover slopes in places such as Chestnut Ridge, where geological conditions are agriculturally marginal.

The soil and the forest at Chestnut Ridge were in fact so complicatedly interdependent that the more one observed them, the more difficulty one had in distinguishing between them. The forest had made the soil, and the soil continually remade the forest from its intricate mosaic of bacteria, fungi, spores, and seeds. The soil lay at the heart of the forest as chromosomes lie at the heart of every living cell, and in this sense the soil *was* the forest—the essential generative stuff that connected it to past and future. It may have seemed easy enough to deny this dual identity by cutting down the forest and planting crops, but there was no assurance that the soil would outlive its parent-offspring in the long run. Agriculture is an extremely recent phenomenon, and the beeches, maples, ashes, hickories, and oaks have been growing on North America for at least sixty million years.

The interdependence of soil and forest was particularly crucial on Chestnut Ridge because the soil was thin. The proximity of bedrock to topsoil was painfully clear where the quarry pits had sectioned the ridgetop. In the deepest pit some twenty feet of mossy, almost unbroken sandstone loomed up from the sunless floor, then another eight feet of weathered and fractured stone above that. Only the top two feet showed a rocky, sandy soil, and only the top few inches of this soil bore the dark stains and organic detritus of humus. It seemed marvelous that the ridgetop trees had sunk roots into this resistant matrix and downright miraculous that a sugar maple sapling had actually managed to grow on the very cliff face. The maple clung to a tiny ledge about four feet below the clifftop, its trunk supported by a fisted clump of roots that snaked over the bare rock before disappearing into cracks.

The creeks ran open for a few days more, then the cold returned—a still, metallic frost that hung over the ridge day after day until the ground was brittle from the ice crystals growing in it. Earthworms and salamanders moved deeper. Mites, springtails, nematodes, protozoans, and fungi froze to death in multitudes—and survived in even greater multitudes by finding sympathetic microclimates or taking refuge in cysts and spores. The chipmunks joined the groundhogs in winter sleep, and the woods were quiet, almost prim. They seemed a little tidier now that the leaf litter was frozen hard and the branches were not disarrayed by warm air currents. Red-bellied woodpeckers and white-breasted nuthatches hitched themselves around the trees making nasal, peevish sounds—spinsters and bachelors in their wintry parlors.

THE SHORTEST DAYS

The doe and her two fawns remained on the ridge through the first two snows, a longer period than other deer had stayed during the year. In the previous, relatively harsh winter, the ridge had been entirely without deer. Perhaps the pregnant doe sensed that the coming winter would be even more harsh and saw in the pine plantations and abandoned orchards good places to find shelter in heavy snows. It was difficult to imagine the motives of the deer: their world of farm woodlots, ravines, cornfields, and suburban backyards was so discontinuous, so frequently disrupted, that one could see little pattern in their movements. In this they were not altogether unlike the people of the countryside —increasingly transient and disorganized, frequently killed or maimed by automobiles, always increasing in numbers.

Their genes still guided them, though. The doe and her fawns had grown fluffy gray coats that made them seem pointy-headed and sheeplike but would keep them alive as they lay sleeping through subzero nights. For food they could browse equally well on soft winter green herbs or prickly red cedar needles. When pressed, they could jump the neighboring suburbanites' fences and eat up their yews and spruces. (Yew is poisonous to humans, but deer will eat every needle off a yew hedge without apparent ill effect.) The massive Herefords on the west slope pastures were not so well equipped for survival. They could endure the cold but would have starved on the yellow grass and multiflora rose thickets of the pastures had not the cattle raiser finally trucked them away to a feedlot.

The first snow that would lie on the ground through the winter fell at midnight two days before the solstice. It was not a heavy snow, and stopped after a few hours. The sky cleared, and the white landscape glittered in the bright dawn. The air was very cold, and the snow did not melt even though there was little more than an inch on the ground. It remained powdery and undiminished through the afternoon, and the glare of sunlight reflected off snow made the ridge seem insubstantial—only the bright blue tree shadows indicated the contours of slopes and gullies. Against the whiteness the quarry cliffs and spring pool resembled black holes more than surfaces of rock or water.

A wind from the southwest blustered through most of the day, raising little cyclones of snow crystals along the ridgetop, baring some spots and burying others in drifts. It filled the tracks left by early morning squirrels and rabbits and kept the songbirds sheltering in thickets. Often the wind was the only thing moving, but some birds seemed to enjoy playing in it. Goldfinches made swift, arching flights above the old fields. Occasionally the wind blew them off course and nearly upended them as surf lifts and rolls swimmers. Mourning doves flew in and out of pine plantations with a headlong clapping of wings, seeming almost able to outrace the wind. The red-tailed hawk pair stilled above the ridge for long moments, facing into the wind so it buoyed up their broad wings, until a strong gust knocked them backward and they had to turn and glide a little before facing it again. It was an easy way to look for meadow mice, although there were few mice to be seen.

The wind died down after an early, almost colorless sunset. The horned owls' calls were very clear in the stillness that followed—the deep "Hoo *hoo* hoo hoo" answered by the higher, excited "Hoo hoo *hoo* hoo hoo." The deep call came from a vine-tangled hickory on the ridgetop, and the last of the short-tailed shrew's autumn litter heard it.

The shrew's heart raced for a moment, but it was safe underground. It had used the warm weather after its mother's death to make new tunnels in the leaf litter and had broken into a carpenter ant's nest in a stump. The sluggish ants, woodlice, beetles, and other inhabitants of the nest had filled its stomach many times, and its condition was much improved. It had the strength to forage and seek new food sources now that the cold weather had returned. It remained timid, reluctant to leave its tunnels, so it didn't emerge to explore the new snow as had its mother a year before.

The owl saw nothing of interest on the ridgetop and flew away to look for mice along the marsh edges. Although the sun had just set, the air was so clear and dry that the winter constellations were out already, Orion in the southeast, Aquarius on the western horizon, the Great Bear low in the north—a polar bear. It was getting very cold indeed.

There was a movement in the maple grove, and the vague,

black outlines of the doe and her fawns came into focus against the starlit snow. They wandered through the grove slowly and silently, raising their heads now and then to smell and listen, lowering them again to nuzzle at herbs uncovered by their hooves. For a little while the deer stood out clearly among the maple trunks, then they drifted by imperceptible degrees into the brush surrounding the grove and were gone.

Future Time

How, then, can our harvest fail? Shall I not rejoice also at the abundance of the weeds whose seeds are the granary of the birds? It matters little comparatively whether the fields fill the farmer's barns. The true husbandman will cease from anxiety, as the squirrels manifest no concern whether the woods will bear chestnuts this year or not, and finish his labor with each day, relinquishing all claim to the produce of his fields, and sacrificing in his mind not only his first but his last fruits also.

Henry Thoreau
Walden

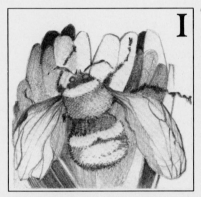

I T HAS become customary when writing about wild places to conclude by speculating on their prospects for survival in a world of ever-expanding human population. Chestnut Ridge is not a dramatically wild place, of course, and its prospects seem correspondingly prosaic. No holocaust of logging, mining, or wildlife slaughter looms on the horizon because these catastrophes have already occurred. Elk and panthers, passenger pigeons and wild turkeys, American chestnuts and elms, ginseng and showy orchids—these assets have already been spent. What remains enjoys some protection as a sylvan retreat for people in the sprawling city to the west. Park roads and picnic areas will certainly leave more of the ridge intact than would a developer's bulldozers.

The landscape architect who is planning the park at Chestnut Ridge thinks it will be a vestige of nature surrounded by subdivisions that will replace the cornfields and pastures now abutting the ridge. He foresees this because he believes in growth and development (those peculiar land speculators' borrowings from the biologists' vocabulary) and because he has seen the subdivisions engulf older parks nearer the city. He may be right, depending on the vagaries of petroleum supplies and the intricacies of economics. If so, the life of the ridge will undergo a further impoverishment.

The flow of deer, foxes, and other errant wildlife over the ridge will be hindered. Red-tailed hawks may not be able to nest with nearby hunting grounds destroyed. Small mammals and ground-nesting birds may be decimated by cats and dogs. There will be population explosions and disease epidemics among the raccoons as they fatten on garbage, breed exuberantly, and are unable to disperse to surrounding habitat. Some of the mature beeches and oaks may die from increased air pollution or from changes in drainage patterns.

But suburbanization will not mean an end to wildness on the ridge any more than the establishment of a park means its salvation. Both these alternatives assume a future completely and permanently under human control, an assumption that is unjustified by present or foreseeable human behavior and is anyway based on a misapprehension of reality. Wildness is not an Eden or Chaos that can be repealed by the extirpation of large wild animals or the removal of forest. It is a fundamental condition of the biosphere.

We have come to think of places such as Chestnut Ridge chiefly as playgrounds or museums, diversions from the reality of getting and spending. Precisely the reverse is true, however: wildness is the workplace of the earth, civilization the playground. The cycling of water, minerals, and gases, which makes life possible, is wild, as are the lesser organisms—bacteria, fungi, algae, protozoans, and invertebrates—which make life possible for the greater. These phenomena are at once too vast and too detailed for any but peripheral human control. Even human bodies and societies defy attempts at control.

When Henry Thoreau wrote "In Wildness is the preservation of the World," he was being as much a Yankee pragmatist as a New England transcendentalist. While implying that the human spirit needs wildness for renewal, he was also asserting that human society—the "World" of history and culture—needs wildness for survival. "The cities import it at any price . . . men plow and sail for it. From the forest and wilderness come the tonics that brace mankind." In this, Thoreau was saying something that every Boston whaler and timber merchant knew well—that there are no products and profits without the raw, wild materials.

Thoreau differed from these practical men only in observing that value cannot lie only in products and profits, and in this he was the truer pragmatist. For it is not really possible that there be "some who can live without wild things and some who cannot." Aldo Leopold was being more poetical than precise when he made this observation. There are some who can live without grouse or maple trees, of course, but there are none who can live without nitrogen-fixing bacteria, pollinating insects, or cellulose-digesting fungi. If asked how these things are wild, one may point out that humans have much less control over their workings than they do over grouse and maple trees.

The abiding value of Chestnut Ridge is its part, however small, in the fundamentally wild process that sustains life. A park at Chestnut Ridge could enhance this value as a link between the human world and the sustaining realm of fields and forests. But as a museum piece surrounded by urban sprawl, the park would amount to a decorative fitting on a sinking ship. Its fabric of beeches, oaks, asters, and goldenrods would become a mere rarity, and its value would decline to that of gold and gems. Important as it is to save rare plants and animals, it is even more important to perpetuate common ones. The fact that there are still thousands of "idle" or gently used places like it engaged in cycling water, minerals, and gases through the biosphere is what gives Chestnut Ridge its main significance, because it is this fact that makes the "World" of human culture possible.

To say that wildness is the preservation of the human world is only the half of it, though. Thoreau could with equal truth have said the opposite: "In Wildness is the destruction of the World." The deteriorative forces that continually tear at civilization are really the same forces that allowed civilization to be made—the global cycling of water, gases, and minerals; the intricate, dynamic fabric of life. They simply come in different forms—as earthquakes, storms, floods, droughts, and pests, instead of fertile soils, gentle rains, blue skies, and honeybees. The fact that many of these destructive forms are abetted by our own activities as we busily pave over watersheds or build on fault zones hardly domesticates them.

The human world is always balanced between the creative and destructive forms of wildness. It is not an enduring monument as it often seems from inside, but a tightrope walk that distributes the forces of nature in the performers' favor as long as they can keep upright. But we come into the world as wild things and go out the same way, no matter how many boxes of lead or concrete we sheath about our bones (and the faster we consume the resources that eons of creative wildness have left us, the faster will the wild forces of deterioration pull us down). So it is not enough to look back and admire wildness as our heritage, we must look forward to it as well. The elk and panthers devoured by our factories and emporiums are presently being excreted as pariah dogs and sewer rats in our inner cities. We may like the new forms even less than our ancestors liked the old, but the pattern is the same.

It is not wildness that is in doubt on Chestnut Ridge but the form wildness will take. Humans have already proved capable of removing the temperate deciduous forest, which seems to be the ridge's preferred form of wildness. Quarrying and deforestation have hurried the ridge's ultimate geological demise considerably. But now the forest is recovering and could within a human generation produce a climax beech, oak, and maple forest that would probably cover the ridge for the rest of its existence, evolving to adapt to whatever climatic or geological conditions might arise meanwhile.

A human civilization that could coexist with some areas of mature forest is conceivable, indeed necessary if any dreams of semiutopian permanence are to come true. Big trees are part of the quality of life, and the only way to have them is to let them grow. But a climax forest on Chestnut Ridge is unlikely if human population and resource consumption continue to explode. The most likely eventuality then (barring the very real possibility of general nuclear or chemical poisoning) would be destruction of the forest by a populace desperate for fuel, the same destruction now taking place in the nonindustrialized world. The ridge would be cut over, probably burned over, then grazed down to the roots. Within a century it would be a scrubby hill frequented by shepherds. There might be a few prolific ashes or slippery elms in gullies; and there would be blackbirds, robins, crows, toads, groundhogs, ironweeds, bluegrass, and a number of other living things; but the ridge would not be as profitable or interesting as it once was, since people are generally better suited to the wildness that made them than to that which they have made. The vast acreage of strip-mined hills that lies east and south of Chestnut Ridge is an example of man-made wild land—good habitat for beetles and broomsedge.

Of course, sheep pasturage wouldn't be the final fate of the ridge. As noted before, its destiny is to be washed down to the sea and redeposited as sedimentary rock. The human population surge has already been more devastating than a million years of glaciation, but it, too, will have its limits and recession. Then a temperate deciduous forest that survived in some obscure place might recolonize the ridge. Short-tailed shrews, box turtles, and yellow-billed cuckoos, or some ecological variants thereof, would perhaps be a part of this forest. There might be some humans, too, and it is interesting to speculate about them because they would probably be as different from us as we are from the mound-building Amerindians.

Prophecy of this kind is really very thin stuff, though. It is always looking for some climax and denouement, while the real future is unlikely to be any more conclusive than the past has been. It's not unlikely that *all* the above-mentioned eventualities will come to pass on Chestnut Ridge, along with a number of unanticipated ones as the continents continue their drift through time. Foresight is generally an exercise in short sight, and the 330 million years of Blackhand sandstone at Chestnut Ridge weigh heavily on ideas of apocalypse and millenium.

Our obsessions with history and prophecy perhaps reflect an inability to comprehend the implications of geological time. The mind's traditional organization of duration into past, present, and future really has more relevance to the five-thousand-year-old earth of the seventeenth century than it does to the five-billion-year-old one of the twentieth. Past and future require certain limitations and symmetries to be meaningful—there must be a plot or at least a story. But time is not really much like a story. It is more like an ocean current that rises from imperfectly perceived depths and flows into unseen distances.

This immensity might seem to diminish the present—the living moment—to utter insignificance, but actually the present looms much larger in geological time than in historical time. If time is a story, the present is merely a hiatus between the significant events that were and will be. If time is an ocean, however, the present is not less important than the other moments, which

168

stretch away on all sides, any more than a single water molecule in an ocean is less important than the others. In a sense each living moment is the whole of time—an eternal present—because it can't be set apart from all the other moments.

The Blackhand sandstone at Chestnut Ridge might be seen as an emblem of this eternal present, since it is pretty much the same today as it was 300 million years ago. All its fixity and duration have not made it more or less significant than the petals of a rue anemone, nor will the addition of another 3 million years to its existence. So it may be best to view the future of the ridge without feeling that it will somehow be more real and permanent than its past and present.

Certainly the ridge will have value as a nature preserve and retreat for future urban people, but it will not be more important than it is at the present moment. Even if the ridge becomes the only green spot in a hundred square miles of skyscrapers, its fundamental value will not be in rarity, in diversion from the human world, but in commonness, in union with the biosphere on which the human world depends. It is in the present moment that the ridge's green plants respire oxygen, catch raindrops, shelter and feed animals, please the eye, and make the soil with their questing roots and fallen leaves. Our future depends on these things.

BIBLIOGRAPHY

Bent, Arthur Cleveland. *Life Histories of North American Birds of Prey*. New York: Dover Press, 1961.

———. *Life Histories of North American Cuckoos, Goatsuckers, Hummingbirds, and Their Allies*. New York: Dover Press, 1964.

———. *Life Histories of North American Jays, Crows, and Titmice*. New York: Dover Press, 1964.

Borror, Donald J., and White, Richard E. *A Field Guide to the Insects of America North of Mexico*. Boston: Houghton Mifflin Company, 1970.

Braun, E. Lucy. *The Woody Plants of Ohio*. Columbus: The Ohio State University Press, 1961.

Brockman, C. Frank. *Trees of North America*. New York: Golden Press, 1968.

Burns, Eugene. *The Sex Life of Wild Animals*. New York: Rinehart & Co., 1953.

Carrighar, Sally. *Wild Heritage*. Boston: Houghton Mifflin Company, 1965.

Conant, Roger. *The Reptiles of Ohio*. Notre Dame, Indiana: The University Press.

Craighead, F. C. *Insect Enemies of Eastern Forests*. Washington, D.C.: U.S. Department of Agriculture, Miscellaneous Publication no. 657, 1950.

Craighead, John C., and Frank C., Jr. *Hawks, Owls, and Wildlife*. New York: Dover Press, 1969.

Dineley, David. *Earth's Voyage Through Time*. New York: Alfred A. Knopf, 1973.

Elliott, Lang. *Social Behavior and Foraging Ecology of the Eastern Chipmunk* (Tamias striatus) *in the Adirondack Mountains*. Smithsonian Contributions to Zoology, no. 265. Washington, D.C.: Smithsonian Institution Press, 1978.

Farb, Peter. *The Living Earth*. New York: Harper, 1959.

Fichter, George S. *Insect Pests*. New York: Golden Press, 1966.

Godfrey, Michael A. *A Closer Look*. San Francisco: Sierra Club Books, 1975.

Gordon, Robert B. *Natural Vegetation of Ohio*. Columbus: Ohio Biological Survey, 1966.

Hamilton, W. J., Jr. "Habits of the Short-Tailed Shrew, *Blarina brevicauda*." *The Ohio Journal of Science*, vol. 31, no. 2, 97-107.

Hanawalt, F. A. "Habits of the Common Mole." *The Ohio Journal of Science*, vol. 22, no. 6, 164-170.

Harper, Arthur R. *Ohio in the Making.* Columbus: The Ohio State University Press, 1948.

Knobel, Edward. *Field Guide to the Grasses, Sedges, and Rushes of the United States.* New York: Dover Press, 1977.

LaRocque, Aurele, and Marple, Mildred Fisher. *Ohio Fossils.* Columbus: Ohio Department of Natural Resources, Division of Geological Survey, Bulletin 54, 1955.

Leopold, Aldo. *A Sand County Almanac.* New York: Oxford University Press, 1949.

Levi, Herbert W. and Lorna R. *A Guide to Spiders and Their Kin.* New York: Golden Press, 1968.

Loomis, Frederick. *Physiography of the United States.* New York: Doubleday, Doran, and Co., Inc., 1938.

Martin, Alexander C. *Weeds.* New York: Golden Press, 1972.

McCormick, Jack. *The Life of the Forest. Our Living World of Nature.* New York: McGraw-Hill, 1966.

Melvin, Ruth V. *A Guide to Ohio Outdoor Education Areas.* Ohio Department of Natural Resources and Ohio Academy of Sciences, 1975.

Miller, William E. "The Goldenrod Gall Moth and Its Parasites in Ohio." *The Ohio Journal of Science,* vol. 63, no. 2, 65-75.

Mitchell, Robert T., and Zim, Herbert S. *Butterflies and Moths: A Guide to the More Common American Species.* New York: Golden Press, 1964.

Morgan, Ann Haven. *Field Book of Ponds and Streams.* New York: G.P. Putnam's Sons, 1930.

Niering, William A. *The Life of the Marsh. Our Living World of Nature.* New York: McGraw-Hill, 1966.

Noble, G. Kingsley. *The Biology of the Amphibia.* New York: Dover Press, 1954.

Peattie, Donald Culross. *A Natural History of the Trees of Eastern and Central North America.* Boston: Houghton Mifflin Company, 1950.

Peterson, Roger Tory. *A Field Guide to the Birds.* Boston: Houghton Mifflin Company, 1947.

Peterson, Roger Tory, and McKenny, Margaret. *A Field Guide to the Wildflowers of Northeastern and North Central North America.* Boston: Houghton Mifflin Company, 1968.

Pope, Clifford H. *Turtles of the United States and Canada.* New York: Alfred A. Knopf, 1971.

Potter, Martha A. *Ohio's Prehistoric Peoples.* Columbus: The Ohio Historical Society, 1968.

Robbins, Chandler S; Bruun, Bertel; and Zim, Herbert S. *Birds of North America.* New York: Golden Press, 1966.

Russell, Franklin. *Watchers at the Pond.* New York: Alfred A. Knopf, 1961.

Schwartz, C. W. and E. R. *The Wild Mammals of Missouri.* Columbia, Missouri: University of Missouri Press and Missouri Conservation Commission, 1959.

Shuttleworth, Floyd S., and Zim, Herbert S. *Non-Flowering Plants*. New York: Golden Press, 1967.

Stauffer, Clinton R.; Hubbard, George D.; and Bownocker, J. A. *Geology of the Columbus Quadrangle*. Columbus: Geological Survey of Ohio, Fourth Series, Bulletin 14, 1911.

Swan, Lester A., and Papp, Charles S. *The Common Insects of North America*. New York: Harper and Row, 1972.

Trautman, Milton B. *The Fishes of Ohio*. Columbus: The Ohio State University Press, 1957.

Walker, Charles F. *Frogs and Toads of Ohio*. Columbus: Ohio State Archaeological and Historical Society, 1946.

Wolfe, Edward W.; Forsyth, Jane L.; and Dove, George D. *Geology of Fairfield County*. Columbus: Ohio Department of Natural Resources, Division of Geological Survey, Bulletin 60, 1962.

GLOSSARY
OF PLANTS AND ANIMALS

Common names of plants and animals are sometimes misleading. This glossary is intended to reduce confusion by providing scientific names of organisms mentioned by common name in the text. Where there is doubt as to the species, names of genus, family, class, or order are given. The number after each entry refers to the first page on which the organism is mentioned, since many appear throughout the book.

Algae, blue green, phylum Cyanophyta. Unicellular or colonial photosynthetic organisms classified in kingdom Monera with bacteria since they are procaryotic (lacking cell nuclei). 75

Algae, filamentous green, division Chlorophyta. Colonial algae that form bright green underwater mats. 75

Alumroot, *Heuchera americana,* saxifrage family. Slightly maple-shaped basal leaves and tall spikes of small, greenish flowers. Eastern United States. 71

Amphipod, order Amphipoda. Scud, sideswimmer. Widely distributed aquatic crustaceans. 94

Aphid, family Aphididae. Plant lice. Small insects that live by sucking plant juices. 77

Aphis, woolly, family Eriostomidae. Closely related to aphids. Produce large amounts of woolly or waxy material. 108

Ash, white, *Fraxinus americana,* olive family. Common ash of eastern deciduous forest. Pinnately compound leaves; fruit a samara. 94

Asparagus, *Asparagus officinalis,* lily family. 58

Aster, heath, *Aster ericoides,* sunflower family. Many small leaves and white or pinkish flowers. Eastern United States. 106

Aster, New England, *Aster novae-angliea.* Large, showy blossoms with violet ray flowers, yellow disk flowers. Lanceolate leaves. Eastern United States and Canada. 119

Aster, white wood, *Aster divericatus.* White blossoms and stalked, heart-shaped leaves. Northeastern United States. 119

Avens, rough, *Geum virginianum,* rose family. Compound leaves with three leaflets; small white or yellow flowers, petals shorter than sepals. 88

Avens, spring, *Geum vernum.* Yellow flowers about one-fourth inch across. Northeastern United States. 21

Bat, big brown, *Eptesicus fuscus.* A large species distributed throughout United States. 150

Bat, red, *Lasiurus borealis.* A large, solitary bat of forests. 145

Bedstraw, genus *Galium,* madder family. Cleavers, goosegrass. Once used to stuff mattresses. 70

Bee, halictid, family Halictidae. Dark-colored or metallic green bees that nest in ground. 49

Bee, honey, family Apidae. This family also includes bumblebees, which, unlike honeybees, are native to North America. 49

Beech, *Fagus grandifolia,* beech family. American beech. Distributed from Nova Scotia to Louisiana on soils with ample surface moisture. 2

Beechdrops, *Epifagus virginiana,* broomrape family. Branching plant with tiny, scalelike leaves. Eastern United States and Canada. Many parasitic plants in this family. 128

Beetle, blister, family Meloidae. Body contains a substance capable of blistering human skin. 35

Beetle, click, family Elateridae. Common group named for ability to click and jump by straightening body suddenly if turned upside down. 30

173

Beetle, ladybird, family Coccinellidae. Lady-
bug. Abundant group of orange, dark-
spotted small beetles. 119

Beetle, locust borer, *Megacyllene robiniae.*
Common black and yellow adults on goldenrod. Larvae feed on black locust by boring in
wood. 122

Beetle, May, family Scarabaeidae, subfamily
Melolonthinae. June beetle. Common heavy-
bodied fliers of early summer nights. 58

Beetle, leaf, *Labidomera clivicollis.* A bluish
black and orange beetle commonly found on
swamp and other milkweeds. 86

Beetle, milkweed longhorn, genus *Tetraopes.*
Long-bodied, red orange beetles with black
spots on back, black legs. 86

Beetle, prionus, genus *Prionus.* Large, broad,
black, or brown beetles. 124

Beetle, red-oak borer, *Prionoxystus robiniae.*
Carpenter worm. Larva also attacks many
other tree species throughout United States.
108

Beetle, rove, family Staphylinidae. Common
beetles that run about quickly with tip of abdomen bent upward. Many are scavengers.
108

Beetle, soldier, family Cantharidae. Slender
beetles, related to fireflies. Often found on
flowers. 77

Beetle, tortoise, family Chrysomelidae, subfamily Cassidinae. Oval, sometimes round
beetles, often gold or silver colored. 49

Beetle, water, families Hydrophilidae, Dytisci-
dae. Water beetles are air-breathers that can
fly from pond to pond. 94

Bellflower, tall, *Campanula americana,* blue-
bell family. Flat, five-lobed blue flowers with
long, curving styles don't resemble bells in
this species. Eastern United States. 88

Bittersweet, *Celastrus scandens,* bittersweet
family. Vine bearing orange pods that split
to reveal scarlet fruit. Commonly used in
decorations. 71

Black-eyed Susan, *Rudbeckia serotina,* sunflower family. Only member of coneflower
genus of prairie and mountain meadow to
turn weedy and invade cultivated areas. 86

Blackberry, genus *Rubus,* rose family. Two
hundred fifty species in eastern United
States. 10

Blackbird, red-winged, *Agelaius phoeniceus.*
Resident or migratory throughout most of
North America except far north. 45

Bloodroot, *Sanguinaria canadensis,* poppy
family. Named for orange-colored juice exuded from broken stem. 6

Blue-eyed grass, genus *Sisyrinchium,* iris family. Grasslike leaves and stems. Blue or white
flowers. 86

Bluegrass, Kentucky, *Poa pratensis,* grass family. Tall perennial with many varieties. Origin uncertain—some varieties introduced,
some apparently native. 71

Bluejay, *Cyanocitta cristata.* Common woodland jay east of Rocky Mountains. 14

Bouncing Bet, *Saponaria officinalis,* pink family. Ragged looking pink or white flowers. 86

Box elder, *Acer negundo,* maple family. Ash-
leaved maple. Pinnately compound leaves
distinguish this from other maples. Most
widespread American maple—California to
New England. 42

Broomsedge, genus *Andropogon,* grass family.
More than thirty species of broomsedge in
United States. 103

Buckeye, *Aesculus glabra,* horse chestnut family. Ohio buckeye. Palmately compound
leaves and glossy brown, poisonous seeds.
Midwestern United States. 145

Bug, leaf, family Miridae. Large group of colorful, plant-feeding bugs. 77

Bug, milkweed, *Oncopeltus fasciatus.* 86

Bug, water, family Belostomidae. Giant water
bug. Predaceous bugs that breathe air and
can fly. 94

Bumblebee, family Apidae. Nest in colonies,
but nests last only one year, unlike honeybees. 49

Bunting, indigo, *Passerina cyanea.* Breeding
male bright blue; female brown. Hedgerows
and wood margins of eastern United States.
65

Burdock, *Arctium minus,* sunflower family.
Coarse, rank-smelling biennial introduced
from Old World. 118

Butterfly, black swallowtail, *Papilio polyxenes.*
Larvae feed on parsley family plants, so also
called parsnip swallowtail. 142

Butterfly, blue, *Celastrina argiolus pseudargi-
olus.* Common blue, spring azure. 52

Butterfly, elfin, genus *Incisalia.* Adults appear
in early spring. 52

Butterfly, falcate orange tip, *Anthocaris midea.*
Another early spring butterfly. Caterpillars
feed on mustard family plants. 52

Butterfly, fritillary, genus *Speyeria.* Large butterflies with speckled orange wings. 103

Butterfly, hackberry, *Asterocampa celtis.* Larvae feed on hackberry trees, as name implies.
30

Butterfly, hairstreak, genus *Strymon.* Hairlike
tails on hind wings and narrow streaks of

color on undersides of wings. Many species. 86

Butterfly, monarch, *Danaus plexippus*. Very common orange, black, and white butterflies. Throughout North America, and have somehow colonized other continents. 86

Butterfly, mourning cloak, *Nymphalis antiopa*. Dark purple with yellow-edged wings. Adults hibernate. 30

Butterfly, pipe-vine swallowtail, *Battus philenor*. 66

Butterfly, question mark, *Polygonia interrogationis*. Name from silvery mark on underside of hind wings. 129

Butterfly, red admiral, *Vanessa atalanta*. Worldwide in North Temperate zone. Larvae feed on nettles. 52

Butterfly, red-spotted purple, *Limenitis astyanax*. Larvae eat mostly wild cherry. 66

Butterfly, sulphur, genus *Colias*. Common yellow butterflies. 129

Butterfly, wood nymph, *Cercyonis pegala*. Common wood nymph. Brown with pale patches marked with dark eyespots. 103

Butterfly weed, *Asclepias tuberosa*, milkweed family. Stems not milky when broken, unlike other milkweeds. 86

Campion, bladder, *Silene cucubalus*, pink family. Inflated, purple veined calyx sack and cleft white petals. 87

Campion, starry, *Silene stellata*. Fringed white petals. 87

Cardinal, *Richmondena cardinalis*. Common crested "redbird" of eastern woodland, south through Mexico to Central America. Mayan word for species is "Chac-tsit-tsib," which seems a good transliteration of its call. 15

Catbird, *Dumetella carolinensis*. Gray relative of mockingbird, named for its mewing call. 65

Caterpillar, leaf miner. Larva of diverse small moths. Some beetle larvae also mine leaves. 109

Caterpillar, tent, *Malacosoma americanum*. Eastern tent caterpillar. Larva of a medium-size, tan-colored moth. 107

Cattail, *Typha latifolia*, cattail family. Broad-leaf cattail and common cattail. Pollen edible. Leaves used as thatching. 15

Centipede, class Diplopoda, order Geophilomorpha. Soil centipede. Slender, eyeless centipedes. 30

Chat, yellow-breasted, *Icteria virens*. Unusually large member of wood warbler family with yellow breast, olive green back. 65

Cherry, black, *Prunus serotina*, rose family. Black, flaky bark and abundant racemes of purple, bittersweet fruit. Wood prized for furniture making. 7

Cherry, mazzard, *Prunus avium*. Cultivated, Old World cherry gone wild. Fruit yellow, red, or black; sweet or sour. 48

Chestnut, American, *Castanea dentata*, beech family. Toothed, lanceolate leaves and prickly burs surrounding nuts. Root sprouts fairly common in Appalachian woods, but most mature specimens long ago killed by blight, an introduced fungus disease. Attempts are being made to develop resistant varieties and reestablish species. 2

Chickadee, Carolina, *Parus carolinensis*. Resembles black-capped chickadee except for whistled song, which sounds like "Oh me, oh my," whereas black-capped's sounds like "Oh my." 15

Chickory, *Cichorium intybus*, sunflower family. Blue sailors. Common roadside weed throughout United States. Seeds used as coffee additive. 86

Chipmunk, *Tamias striatus*. Eastern chipmunk. Common striped burrowing squirrel of eastern forest. 36

Chive, wild, genus *Allium*, lily family. Wild garlic. 141

Cicada, family Cicadidae. Blackish, green-marked insects described here are a different species from periodical cicadas, which only emerge as adults every thirteen to seventeen years. 30

Cinquefoil, genus *Potentilla*, rose family. White or yellow, five-petaled flowers and five- or three-parted leaves. 71

Clover, red, *Trifolium pratense*, pea family. 60

Cockroach, woodland, family Blattidae. There are a few species of these ancient insects native to the northern United States. 85

Coneflower, green-headed, *Rudbeckia laciniata*, sunflower family. Named for greenish disk flowers. 119

Copepod, order Copepoda. Tiny crustaceans of shallow water. *Cyclops* is a common genus. 94

Cottonwood, *Populus deltoides*, willow family. Eastern cottonwood. Named for cottony hairs on seeds. 115

Cowbird, brown-headed, *Molothrus ater*. Same family as red-winged blackbird. 71

Crayfish, order Decapoda. *Cambarus bartoni* is a common stream species. *Cambarus diogenes* lives in marshes, builds "chimney" burrows. 94

Cricket, bush, family Gryllidae, subfamily Trigonidiinae, 97

Cricket, camel, family Gryllacrididae. Brownish, humpbacked crickets of dark places. 115

Cricket, field, family Gryllidae, subfamily Gryllinae. Common blackish crickets, including house cricket, an introduced species. 73

Cricket, ground, family Gryllidae, subfamily Nemobiinae. Common crickets, but small and seldom noticed. 84

Cricket, mole, family Gryllidae, subfamily Gryllotalpinae. Head and shovellike front legs surprisingly molelike. Burrows underground. 18

Cricket, tree, family Gryllidae, subfamily Oecanthinae. Slender crickets of trees and bushes. High-pitched chirps or trills. 90

Crow, *Corvus brachyrhynchos*. Common crow. Numbers have decreased markedly in recent years. 14

Cuckoo, yellow-billed, *Coccyzus americanus*. Summer breeder where forest available in all but northernmost parts of United States. 65

Cuckoo, black-billed, *Coccyzus erythropthalmus*. Summer breeder in northeastern United States. Red skin around eye of adult. 76

Cutgrass, rice, *Leersia oryzoides*, grass family. Saw-toothed leaves and feathery seed clusters. Wet places in most of North America. 93

Dace, redbelly, *Chrosomus erythrogaster*. Bellies of males turn red during spring spawning season. Dark stripe along side. Common eastern minnow. 54

Daisy, oxeye, *Chrysanthemum leucanthemum*, sunflower family. Field daisy. White ray flowers and yellow disk flowers. 86

Dame's rocket, *Hesperis matronalis*, mustard family. Four-petaled, pink, purple, or white flowers. 63

Darter, family Percidae. Dozens of species of these colorful bottom-dwelling relatives of yellow perch in eastern United States, including famous snail darter of Tellico Dam. 83

Deer, white-tailed, *Odocoileus virginianus*. Throughout North America except far north, Pacific coast, Great Basin. 15

Deptford pink, *Dianthus armeria*, pink family. Slender meadow plant with small, five-petaled flowers. 86

Diatoms, order Diatomaceae. Siliceous, single-celled algae. 94

Dogbane, *Apocynum cannabinum*, dogbane family. Indian hemp. Milkweedlike plants with greenish white flowers. Name refers to alleged use as drug by Indians. 77

Dogwood, *Cornus florida*, dogwood family. Flowering dogwood. Eastern United States. Showy white "petals" actually bracts. 67

Dove, mourning, *Zenaidura macroura*. Named for mournful call. 160

Earthworm, phylum Annelidae, class Oligochaeta, genus *Lumbricus*. 18

Earwig, order Dermaptera. Slender, flattened insects with forcepslike cerci at rear of abdomen. Name comes from superstition that they crawl into people's ears. 63

Elk, *Cervus canadensis*. Wapiti, red deer. Formerly ranged over most of North America; now mainly in western mountains. 164

Elm, American, *Ulmus americana*, elm family. Formerly a dominant species of eastern deciduous forest, now decimated by Dutch elm disease, a fungus. 164

Elm, slippery, *Ulmus rubra*. Smaller than American elm; a common second-growth species. Bark once chewed to relieve sore throat; still used for patent medicines. 40

Fairy shrimp, order Anostraca. About twenty-five species of these upside-down-swimming crustaceans in North America. 43

False Solomon's seal, *Smilacina racemosa*, lily family. Trailing plants with pointed, oval leaves and terminal flower clusters. 58

Fawn lily, *Erythronium americanum*, lily family. Trout lily, adder's tongue, dogtooth violet. Mottled leaves and reflexed yellow petals. 41

Fern, Christmas, *Polystichum acrostichoides*. Common evergreen fern of eastern woods. 149

Firefly, family Lampyridae. Lightning bug. Luminous beetles common throughout eastern United States. 73

Fishfly, order Megaloptera. Tan-colored relatives of dobsonflies and alderflies. Larvae predaceous. 44

Fleabane, daisy, *Erigeron annuus*, sunflower family. Name refers to alleged flea-repellent properties. 71

Flicker, common, *Colaptes auratus*. Brown and gray woodpecker common throughout United States. Eastern race has yellow on undersides of wings. 127

Fly, black, family Simuliidae. Small, stocky flies. Females bite painfully. 74

Fly, bluebottle, family Calliphoridae. Blowfly. Large group of often metallic blue or green flies. Larvae feed on dead matter. 79

Fly, crane, family Tipulidae. Resemble giant mosquitoes, but don't bite humans. 30

Fly, deer, family Tabanidae, genus *Chrysops*. Horseflies also classified in this hard-biting family. 74

Fly, phantom crane, family Ptychopteridae. Swampy habitats. 129

Fly, snipe, family Rhagionidae. Long-legged flies of woodland areas. 74

Fly, syrphid, family Syrphidae. Common flies, many resembling bees or wasps; they don't sting, however. 49

Fox, gray, *Urocyon cinereoargenteus.* Common fox of brush and forest throughout Americas south of Canada. Gray fur with white throat; feet and legs rusty. 37

Fox, red, *Vulpes fulva.* Reddish yellow fur with white underparts, black legs and feet. Most of North America north of Mexico. 27

Frog, green, *Rana clamitans.* Nova Scotia to North Carolina, west to Minnesota, and introduced in West. 54

Frog, striped chorus, *Pseudacris triseriata.* Tiny brown or greenish frogs with three dark stripes on back. Grassy areas with spring breeding pools. 43

Frog, wood, *Rana sylvatica.* Color varies from pink to black. Ranges north to Canadian tundra. Often starts calling when ice still on ponds in late winter. 43

Fungus, artist's, *Ganoderma applanatum.* A large bracket fungus, flat undersurface of which has been used as a "canvas" by artists. 104

Fungus, black-spot, *Venturia inaequalis.* Apple scab. Major disease of orchards. 109

Geranium, wild, *Geranium maculatum,* geranium family. Five-parted leaves, five-petaled flowers. 52

Ginseng, *Panax quinquefolius,* ginseng family. Five-parted, palmate leaves and clusters of red berries. Has been extirpated from many areas by collectors of valuable root. 164

Gnatcatcher, blue gray, *Polioptila caerulea.* Summer breeder in most of eastern United States. 49

Goatsbeard, *Tragopogon pratensis,* sunflower family. Yellow flowers close at midday. Grasslike leaves. 71

Goldenrod, blue-stemmed, *Solidago caesia,* sunflower family. Tufts of yellow flowers spaced along leaf axils of bluish green stem.

Goldenrod, Canada, *Solidago canadensis.* Yellow flowers in plumelike cluster at top of plant. 119

Goldenrod, lance-leaved, *Solidago graminifolia.* Flowers in flat-topped cluster. 106

Goldfinch, *Spinus tristis.* American goldfinch. Yellow-bodied, black-winged finch of weedy fields throughout contiguous United States. 65

Grackle, *Quiscalus quiscula.* Common grackle. Iridescent black plumage may be bluish, greenish, or violet. Eastern United States. 38

Grape, wild, genus *Vitis,* grape family. Many species in eastern forests. Old vines may be as thick as a man's leg. 10

Grasshopper, family Acrididae. Short-horned grasshopper. A large family containing the common, daytime grasshoppers of meadows and fields. 81

Grasshopper, cone-headed, family Tettigoniidae, subfamily Copiphorinae. Slender relatives of katydids. Cone-shaped heads. 90

Grasshopper, long-horned, family Tettigoniidae. 96

Grasshopper, meadow, family Tettigoniidae, subfamily Conocephalinae. Mainly in wet, grassy places. 129

Ground ivy, *Glechoma hederacea,* mint family. Gill-over-the-ground. Creeping plant with rounded, scalloped leaves and violet flowers in whorls. 28

Groundhog, *Marmota monax.* Woodchuck. Northeastern states, then northwest across Canada to central Alaska. Large, burrowing member of squirrel family. 9

Hackberry, *Celtis occidentalis,* elm family. Warty gray bark and small, sweet purple fruits. 2

Harvestman, order Opiliones. Daddy longlegs. Related to spiders, but lack web-spinning ability. 84

Hawk, Cooper's *Accipiter cooperi.* A short-winged forest hawk with blue gray back, rusty breast. 121

Hawk, red-shouldered, *Buteo lineatus.* Woodland soaring hawk of eastern states, California. 38

Hawk, red-tailed, *Buteo jamaicensis.* Commonest soaring hawk of North America. Broad wings, rounded tail. Eastern race tends to pale coloring. 15

Hawk, sharp-shinned, *Accipiter striatus.* Jay-size. Plumage resembles that of Cooper's hawk. 27

Hawthorn, genus *Crataegus,* rose family. Over

one hundred species in North America. Branches often spiny. 117

Hemlock, water, *Cicuta maculata,* parsley family. Swamp hemlock. Umbels of white flowers, compound leaves. 139

Hickory, bitternut, *Carya cordiformis,* walnut family. Compound leaves with seven to eleven leaflets. Smooth bark. 131

Hickory, shagbark, *Carya ovata.* Compound leaves with five to nine leaflets. Sweet nuts. 131

Honey locust, *Gleditsia triacanthos,* pea family. Large pods contain sweet orange pulp. Branches armed with sharp spines. 45

Honeysuckle, Japanese, *Lonicera japonica,* honeysuckle family. A weedy Asian vine that has overwhelmed and smothered a large acreage of second-growth eastern woodland. 10

Hop hornbeam, *Ostrya virginiana,* birch family. Ironwood. Fruits resemble hops; wood very hard. 128

Hornet, bald-faced, family Vespidae, subfamily Vespinae. Yellow jackets belong to same group. 152

Horsetail, genus *Equisetum.* Whorls of slender branchlets make these primitive fern allies look like horses' tails. Wet, sandy places worldwide. 94

Hummingbird, ruby-throated, *Archilochus colubris.* Only breeding hummingbird east of Great Plains. 63

Ironweed, genus *Vernonia,* sunflower family. 77

Jack-in-the-pulpit, *Arisaema atrorubens,* arum family. Odd green and purple flowering structure inspired peculiar name. 118

Jerusalem artichoke, *Helianthus tuberosus,* sunflower family. Edible tubers on roots. 118

Jewelweed, *Impatiens capensis,* touch-me-not family. Spotted touch-me-not. Orange, pendant blossoms spotted with dark orange. Another common species, *I. pallida,* has yellow flowers. 45

Junco, *Junco hyemalis.* Dark-eyed junco. Most of United States. Eastern race, formerly called slate-colored junco, has gray head and back. 15

Katydid, angular-winged, family Tettigoniidae, genus *Microcentrum.* 96

Katydid, bush, family Tettigoniidae, genus *Scudderia.* 96

Katydid, true, family Tettigoniidae, subfamily Pseudophyllinae. Mainly eastern in distribution. 96

Kidneyleaf crowfoot, *Ranunculus abortivus,* buttercup family. Basal leaves kidney-shaped; stem leaves shaped like a crow's foot. 21

Kingbird, eastern, *Tyrannus tyrannus.* Red streak on top of head. East of Great Plains. 64

Kinglet, golden-crowned, *Regulus satrapa.* Bright red, gold, and black striped head on breeding male. Nests in conifers. 49

Knotweed, Virginia, *Tovara virginiana,* buckwheat family. Broad leaves; tiny flowers hugging wiry stem. 88

Lacewing, family Chrysopidae. Green lacewing. Common predator of aphids. 85

Ladies' tresses, slender, *Spiranthes gracilis,* orchid family. White, green-spotted flowers arranged spirally on single stem, like braided hair. 119

Larkspur, dwarf, *Delphinium tricorne,* buttercup family. Spring larkspur. Spurred flowers and deeply cleft leaves. 13

Leek, wild, *Allium tricoccum,* lily family. Northeast and Appalachia. 92

Locust, black, *Robinia pseudoacacia,* pea family. Widely planted on strip mines or other erosion-prone soils because roots contain nitrogen-fixing bacteria. 8

Loosestrife, yellow, *Lysimachia quadrifolia,* primrose family. Whorled loosestrife. Five-petaled yellow flowers in whorls on leaf axils. 86

Maple, red, *Acer rubrum,* maple family. Southern Florida to northern Quebec. 139

Maple, silver, *Acer saccharinum.* Grows rapidly, so often planted in suburbs. 52

Maple, sugar, *Acer saccharum.* Sweet sap, very hard wood. 7

Marijuana, *Cannabis sativa,* mulberry family. Indian hemp. Used for making rope as well as for a drug. Has escaped from cultivation in many places. 78

Mayapple, *Podophyllum peltatum,* barberry family. Flower in crotch between two large, umbrellalike leaves. 45

Midge, family Chironomidae. Common, tiny flies found almost everywhere. Larvae aquatic, adults form large breeding swarms. 145

Mildew, class Phycomycetes. A large group of microscopic fungi. Downy white mildew is made up of sporangia, fruiting bodies of fungus. 104

Mildweed, common, *Asclepias syriaca,* milkweed family. Broad leaves, warty pods. 86

Mildweed, swamp, *Asclepias incarnata.* Narrow leaves, smooth pods. 86

Millipede, class Diplopoda. Differs from centipede in having two pairs of legs on each body segment instead of one pair. 30

Mink, *Mustela vison.* A dark brown, aquatic weasel relative found along streams and lakes in most of North America north of Mexico. 29

Mite, chigger, family Trombiculidae. Harvest mite. Adults are predators on insects; larvae are parasitic, in some species on humans. 74

Mite, oribatid, suborder Sarcoptiformes. Beetle mites. Several families of mites with hard, shiny shells. 30

Mite, water, superfamily Hydrachnellae. Several families of colorful aquatic mites. 44

Mole, eastern, *Scalopus aquaticus.* Moist, loamy soils in most of eastern United States. 54

Monkeyflower, *Mimulus ringens,* snapdragon family. Lobed, violet lips of flowers suggest monkey face. 94

Morel, genus *Morchella.* Fungus producing stalked fruiting bodies with spongy, conical heads. One species may cause illness, but most edible and highly prized. Related to truffles. 57

Mosquito, treehole, genus *Aedes.* Larvae live in water-filled holes in trees. Adults have dark bands on legs. 74

Moss, cushion, *Leucobryum glaucum.* Forms cushionlike mats on poor, acid soil. 149

Moss, haircap, *Polytrichum commune.* Spore cover resembles small, hairy cap. 149

Moth, bagworm, family Psychidae. Small, stout-bodied moths, female usually wingless. 149

Moth, cecropia, *Hyalophora cecropia.* Spectacularly large, reddish gray moths with showy markings. 66

Moth, codling, *Carpocapsa pomonella.* Larva is the common "worm in the apple." 47

Moth, luna, *Actias luna.* An unmistakable green moth with swallow-tailed hind wings. 84

Moth, maple spanworm, *Prochoerodes transversata.* Larvae resemble twigs, adults dead leaves. 47

Moth, mildweed tiger, *Euchaetias egle.* Larvae much showier than gray adults. 66

Moth, noctuid, family Noctuidae. Owlet moth. Commonest moths. 34

Moth, pale tiger, *Halisidota tesselaris.* 109

Moth, royal leopard, *Ecpantheria scribonia.*

Great leopard moth. Adults have white wings marked with black spots. 66

Moth, tiger, *Callarethia virgo.* Orange and black wings. 85

Mouse, deer, *Peromyscus maniculatus.* Big-eyed, big-eared mouse of forest or grassland from Midwest to Alaska. Tail white below, dark above. 26

Mouse, meadow, *Microtus pennsylvanicus.* Meadow vole. Northeastern United States to Alaska. Small-eyed, small-eared, short-tailed mouse of grassy places. 34

Mouse, white-footed, *Peromyscus leucopus.* East and Midwest. Looks like deer mouse, but tail not always bicolored and prefers woodland. 113

Mushroom, genus *Marasmius.* Gill fungus bearing tiny mushrooms, including some that form "fairy rings" of mushrooms in grassy places. 104

Mushroom, genus *Russula.* Common genus of gill fungi, often with bright-colored mushroom caps. Some edible. 104

Muskrat, *Ondatra zibethica.* Aquatic rodents of wetlands in most of North America south of Mexico. Fur of major economic importance. 15

Nematode, phylum Nematoda. Large phylum of parasitic or free-living roundworms. 30

Nighthawk, *Chordeiles minor.* Common nighthawk. Soaring flight—usually at dusk—resembles a true hawk's, but there the relationship ends. Nasal "peent" call resembles woodcock's. 121

Nuthatch, white-breasted, *Sitta carolinensis.* Gray back, black scalp, white face and breast. Nasal "yank, yank" call common in woods throughout contiguous United States. 15

Oak, black, *Quercus velutina,* beech family. Bristle-tipped, five- to seven-lobed leaves and black bark. Acid hill soils. 2

Oak, red, *Quercus rubra.* Northern red oak. Seven- to eleven-lobed leaves resemble black oak's. 152

Oak, scarlet, *Quercus coccinea.* Five- to seven-lobed, bristle-tipped leaves more slender than black or red oak's. Turns scarlet in fall. 2

Oak, white, *Quercus alba.* Leaves have seven to nine rounded (not bristle-tipped) lobes. Pale gray bark in narrow vertical plates. 139

Opossum, *Didelphis marsupialis.* Name from an Algonkian Indian term meaning "white animal." Only marsupial in United States. 23

Orchard grass, *Dactylis glomerata,* grass family. Perennial, common hay crop. 71

Osprey, *Pandion haliaetus.* Fish hawk. Seen inland only during migration. 121

Ovenbird, *Seiurus aurocapillus.* Brown, speckle-breasted wood warbler with orange cap. Domed nest on forest floor resembles old-fashioned outdoor bread oven. 64

Owl, barred, *Strix varia.* Swamps and woodlands throughout eastern United States. Distinguished from screech and great horned owl by dark eyes, lack of "ears." 24

Owl, great horned, *Bubo virginianus.* Large "eared" owl common throughout North America, except Arctic tundra. 14

Owl, screech, *Otus asio.* Small "eared" owl found throughout contiguous United States. 14

Panther, *Felis concolor.* Puma, mountain lion, cougar. Only remaining eastern populations in southern swamps, possibly northern Appalachians. 164

Passenger pigeon, *Ectopistes migratorius.* Numbered in billions before 1800; extinct soon after 1900. 6

Pawpaw, *Asimina triloba,* custard apple family. Small tree with large leaves. 57

Pewee, wood, *Contopus virens.* Eastern wood pewee. Whistled song sounds like name. A medium-size, brownish flycatcher of mature woodland. 110

Phlox, wild blue, *Phlox divaricata,* phlox family. Opposite leaves; flowers radiate from tip of stem. 52

Phoebe, eastern, *Sayornis phoebe.* Medium-size flycatcher that prefers to nest on cliffs, bridges, or buildings. 49

Pickerel, grass, *Esox americanus.* Mud pickerel, barred pickerel. Maximum length one foot. Small streams and swamps. 83

Pine, white, *Pinus strobus,* pine family. Eastern white pine. Widely planted outside natural range as timber and shelter tree. 39

Plantain, water. *Alisma triviale,* arrowhead family. Emergent swamp plant with many-branched stems of small white flowers; ovate leaves. 94

Poison ivy, *Rhus radicans,* sumac family. Trifoliate, compound leaves; white berries. May grow as shrub or as vine, clinging to tree trunks with hairy, aerial roots. 10

Protozoan, phylum Protozoa. Acellular or unicellular animals. 94

Puffball, *Lycoperdon pyriforme.* Pear shaped. Grows in clumps on decaying wood. 104

Queen Anne's lace, *Daucus carota,* parsley family. Wild carrot. Domestic carrot is same species. 86

Quail, bobwhite, *Colinus virginianus.* Common quail of eastern farmland. Call sounds like "Bob bob white!" 23

Rabbit, cottontail, *Sylvilagus floridanus.* Eastern cottontail. 25

Raccoon, *Procyon lotor.* Common name from Algonkian Indian term meaning "the feeler." Most of contiguous United States, except deserts. 15

Ragwort, golden, *Senecio aureus,* sunflower family. Yellow disk and ray flowers; heart-shaped, long-stalked leaves. 57

Redbud, *Cercis canadensis,* pea family. Eastern redbud. Heart-shaped leaves and showy blossoms. 48

Red cedar, *Juniperus virginiana,* cedar family. Eastern red cedar. Foliage spiky on new branches, scaly on old. Cones like blue "berries." 149

Redstart, American, *Setophaga ruticilla.* Black and orange wood warbler of deciduous forests. 63

Robin, *Turdus migratorius,* American robin. Nests from Texas to Alaska. 28

Rose, multiflora, *Rosa multiflora,* rose family. Many small white blossoms. Grows in dense, weedy clumps. Introduced as a hedge plant but has become a common wild species. 68

Rose, swamp, *Rosa palustris.* Bushy plant with pink, yellow-stamened blossoms. 93

Rose, wild, *Rosa carolina.* Pasture rose. Low, slender plant with pink, yellow-stamened blossoms. 86

Rue anemone, *Anemonella thalictroides,* buttercup family. White or pinkish blossoms above whorl of small, three-lobed leaves. 42

Running ground pine, *Lycopodium complanatum.* Club moss common in temperate regions of both hemispheres. 149

Rush, family Juncaceae. Cylindrical-stemmed, herbaceous monocots of moist ground. 93

Salamander, red-backed, *Plethodon cinereus.* Most fallen logs in northeastern woods will have these little batrachians living under them. 135

Salamander, slimy, *Plethodon glutinosus.* Eastern United States. 135

Salamander, spotted, *Ambystoma maculatum.* Nova Scotia to Texas. 35

Sassafras, *Sassafras albidum,* laurel family. Leaves may be elliptical or two to three lobed. Bark and root oils used in beverages and soap. 57

Scorpionweed, *Phacelia purshii*, waterleaf family. Miami mist. Pinnately cleft leaves. 67

Shrew, short-tailed, *Blarina brevicauda*. Eastern United States. 17

Skipper, silver-spotted, *Epargyreus clarus*. Skippers look like small butterflies but have differently shaped antennae. 52

Skullcap, genus *Scutellaria*, mint family. Many species. 88

Skunk, *Mephitis mephitis*. Striped skunk. Most of North America. 9

Slug, class Gastropoda. Similar to snails but without shell. 35

Smartweed, genus *Polygonum*, buckwheat family. Swelling and sheath on stem at each leaf joint. Common name from irritating juice in stems. Many species. 129

Snail, land, class Gastropoda. 35

Snake, black, *Elaphe obsoleta*. Black rat snake. A large constrictor; often climbs trees. Usually shiny black but sometimes spotted. 125

Snake, garter, *Thamnophis sirtalis*, eastern garter snake. Usually yellowish stripes may be brownish, greenish, or bluish. Most common snake. 125

Snake, water, *Natrix sipedon*. Northern water snake. Gray or brown snakes marked with reddish brown or black. Aggressive when provoked, but nonpoisonous. 125

Snakeroot, white, *Eupatorium rugosum*, sunflower family. Heart-shaped, stalked leaves and white flower heads. 106

Sparrow, field, *Spizella pusilla*. Common in eastern United States. Pink bill and legs. 33

Sparrow, song, *Melospiza melodia*. Moist places in most of North America. Sings most of year. 15

Sparrow, swamp, *Melospiza georgiana*. Bogs and marshes of eastern United States and Canada. 15

Sparrow, tree, *Spizella arborea*. A rusty-capped sparrow forming large flocks in winter. Nests in northern Canada. 156

Sparrow, white-throated, *Zonotrichia albicollis*. Head black and white striped, with yellow spot in front of eye. Song transcribed as "Old Sam Peabody Peabody Peabody." 138

Spicebush, *Lindera benzoin*, laurel family. Aromatic leaves and twigs have been used to make a tea. 48

Spider, *Argiope aurantia*. Garden spider. 123

Spider, arrow-shaped micrathena, *Micrathena sagittata*. Eastern United States. 96

Spider, crab, family Thomisidae. Colorful spiders that hold their legs out to the sides crab-fashion and wait in ambush for insects. 49

Spider, jumping, *Phidippus audax*, droll, hairy daytime spiders. This species common on meadow or prairie vegetation east of Rocky Mountains. 86

Spider, sheetweb weaver, subfamily Linyphiinae. 103

Spider, spined micrathena, *Micrathena gracilis*, Eastern United States. 96

Spider, genus *Verrucosa*. 95

Spider, white micrathena, *Micrathena mitrata*. Eastern United States. 96

Spider, wolf, family Lycosidae. Gray or brown spiders that pursue prey on ground. 34

Spleenwort, ebony, *Asplenium platyneuron*, Stiff, slender dark green fern of eastern North America. 149

Spring beauty, *Claytonia virginica*, purslane family. Linear leaves; five-petaled white flowers veined with pink. Small edible tubers. 6

Spring peeper, *Hyla crucifer*. Color varies from brown to olive but dark X shape on back usually identifies this small treefrog. 43

Springtail, order Collembola. Populations can number in the millions per acre. 29

Squawroot, *Conopholis americana*, broomrape family. Scalelike leaves and lack of green pigment. 88

Squirrel, fox, *Sciurus niger*. Midwestern fox squirrels are rusty gray with orange underparts and tail. Species has different pelage in south and east. 27

Squirrel, gray, *Sciurus carolinensis*. Eastern gray squirrel. Smaller than fox squirrel but more numerous and agressive in towns and extensive woodlands. Occasional mass migrations. 22

Squirrel, red, *Tamiasciurus hudsonicus*. Northeast and Appalachians to Alaska and Rockies. Conifers or bottomland hardwoods. 22

Starling, *Sturnus vulgaris*. Introduced from Europe in nineteenth century; now most of North America. 55

Sunflower, woodland, *Helianthus divaricatus*, sunflower family. Dry woods and thickets of eastern United States. 119

Sweet cicely, *Osmorhiza longistylis*, parsley family. Stems smooth; fernlike leaves. Licorice smell. 21

Sweet cicely, hairy, *Osmorhiza claytoni*. Similar to above, except stem hairy. 67

Swift, chimney, *Chaetura pelagica*. Roosts and nests in chimneys or hollow trees. Related to hummingbirds, despite resemblance to swallows. 106

Sycamore, *Platanus occidentalis*, sycamore family. American sycamore. White, tan, and olive mottled bark unmistakable. Leaves maple shaped. Trunk circumference can grow to over thirty feet on fertile bottomland. 7

Tanager, scarlet, *Piranga olivacea*. Breeding male bright scarlet with black wings and tail. Female and winter male yellow green. 63

Teasel, *Dipsacus sylvestris*, teasel family. Spiny heads packed with small lavender flowers. Paired leaves embrace stem, catch water after rain. 86

Thistle, Canada, *Cirsium arvense*, sunflower family. Spindly thistles with many branches of small purple flower heads. 77

Thrush, hermit, *Hylocichla guttata*. Nests in northern and western conifers. Grayish brown plumage; exquisite, flutelike song. 130

Thrush, Swainson's, *Hylocichla ustulata*. Grayish thrush with rolling, flutelike song, rising up scale. Northern woodlands. 130

Thrush, wood, *Hylocichla mustelina*. Brown, speckle-breasted thrush of eastern deciduous forests. 63

Tick, wood, *Dermacentor variabilis*. Brown tick with whitish markings. Eastern United States. 74

Timothy, *Phleum pratense*, grass family. Common perennial hay grass with spikelike flower heads. 132

Titmouse, tufted, *Parus bicolor*. Crested, gray relative of chickadee. Eastern woodlands. 15

Toad, American, *Bufo americanus*. Common eastern toad. 53

Toothwort, cutleaf, *Dentaria laciniata*, mustard family. Whorls of three leaves, each divided in three ragged segments. White or violet flowers. 41

Towhee, rufous-sided, *Pipilo erythropthalmus*. Calls "chewink." Brushy places in most of United States. Black back, reddish sides, white breast. Eyes of adults usually red. 15

Treehopper, family Membracidae. Small jumping relatives of cicadas. 152

Trefoil, tick, genus *Desmodium*, pea family. Sticktight, beggarweed. Eastern states. 106

Trillium, large-flowered, *Trillium grandiflorum*, lily family. White trillium. Eastern United States. 48

Tulip tree, *Liriodendron tulipfera*, magnolia family. Yellow poplar. Four-lobed leaves and flowers resembling greenish yellow and orange tulips. To 150 feet tall. 8

Turkey, *Meleagris gallopavo*. Originally found throughout eastern forests; now reintroduced in much of Appalachian Plateau. 164

Turtle, box, *Terrapene carolina*. Eastern box turtle. Southern New England to Illinois, Georgia. 51

Turtle, snapping, *Chelydra serpentina*. United States east of the Great Plains. 44

Viburnum, genus *Viburnum*, honeysuckle family. Many species. 117

Violet, pale white, *Viola strata*, violet family. Cream violet. Leaves and flowers on same stalk. 48

Violet, smooth yellow, *Viola pennsylvanica*. Leaves and flowers on same stalk. 48

Violet, wild blue, *Viola papilionacae*. Leaves and flowers on separate stalk. 21

Vireo, white-eyed, *Vireo griseus*. Common but inconspicuous in eastern thickets. 65

Vireo, red-eyed, *Vireo olivaceus*. Most abundant bird of eastern deciduous forests, but spends most of time in treetops so not often seen. Olive green back, white breast and eye stripe. 72

Virginia creeper, *Parthenocissus quinquefolia*, grape family. Vine with palmate, five-parted compound leaves. 13

Vulture, turkey, *Cathartes aura*. Resident or migratory throughout contiguous United States, except New England. 45

Walkingstick, family Phasmatidae. Bizarre wingless relative of crickets and katydids. Feeds on plants. Mostly in tropics. 127

Walnut, black, *Juglans nigra*, walnut family. Delicious nuts, but extremely hard to crack. Wood very valuable. 120

Warbler, black and white, *Mniotilta varia*. Only wood warbler that feeds on tree trunks nuthatch-fashion. 63

Warbler, black-throated blue, *Dendroica caerulescens*. Black throat, blue back, white breast on breeding male. 130

Warbler, Blackburnian, *Dendroica fusca*. Only wood warbler with fiery orange throat plumage (on breeding male). 63

Warbler, blackpoll, *Dendroica striata*. Breeding male has black crown, white cheeks and throat. 130

Warbler, blue-winged, *Vermivora pinus*. Yellow breast and head, bluish gray wings barred with white. 65

Warbler, magnolia, *Dendroica magnolia.* Yellow throat, white band on black tail. 130

Warbler, prairie, *Dendroica discolor.* Nests in old fields with deciduous saplings, not prairies. Yellow breast, black-streaked sides, olive back. 65

Warbler, yellow-rumped, *Dendroica coronata.* Perhaps most commonly seen warbler. Yellow patches on scalp and shoulders of breeding males as well as on rump. 49

Water boatman, family Corixidae. Common underwater bug. Swims using legs oar-fashion. 44

Water strider, family Gerridae. Common surface-skating bug. 144

Waterleaf, large-leaved. *Hydrophyllum macrophyllum,* waterleaf family. Rough, hairy plants with five- to seven-lobed leaves marked as though stained with water. White flowers with long protruding stamens. 67

Waterleaf, Virginia, *Hydrophyllum virginianum.* Similar to above, but plants smooth. 88

Whippoorwill, *Caprimulgus vociferus.* Eastern United States. Nests on ground. 90

Willow, genus *Salix,* willow family. Over one hundred species in North America, mostly similar in general appearance. 42

Wingstem, *Actinomeris alternifolia,* sunflower family. Winglike flanges on stem. 93

Woodcock, *Philohela minor.* American woodcock. Inland sandpiper of moist eastern woods and swamps. 34

Woodlice, order Isopoda. Sow bugs, pill bugs. Terrestrial crustaceans, abundant under fallen logs. 115

Woodpecker, downy, *Dendrocopus pubescens.* Commonest eastern woodpecker, with range also extending to west and Alaska. Black and white except for red patch on back of head. 15

Woodpecker, pileated, *Dryocopus pileatus.* Red crest, solid black back. 22

Woodpecker, red-bellied, *Centurus carolinus.* Red cap, black and white "ladder" pattern on back. Belly not noticeably red. Eastern woods south of New York. 22

Woodpecker, red-headed, *Melanerpes erythrocephalus.* Open deciduous woods of eastern United States. Head completely red, white breast, black back. 141

Wren, Carolina, *Thryothorus ludovicianus.* Largest eastern wren. Broad white eye stripe, reddish brown back, buffy underparts. 22

Wren, house, *Troglodytes aedon.* Common around buildings with adjacent woods across north and central United States. Aggressive nesting habits may drive away other hole-nesting species such as bluebirds. 71

Yellow rocket, *Barbarea vulgaris,* mustard family. Winter cress. 60

Yellowthroat, *Geothlypis trichas.* Yellow throat and breast, olive back; black mask on male. Common wood warbler of moist grassy or shrubby areas throughout United States. 65